THE OFFICIAL
LaStone Therapy
MANUAL

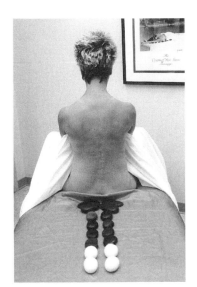

Other Books by Jane Scrivner

THE OFFICIAL
LaStone Therapy
MANUAL

MARY NELSON WITH JANE SCRIVNER

piatkus

PIATKUS

First published in Great Britain in 2004 by Piatkus
Reprinted 2008, 2009, 2011

A CIP catalogue record for this book
is available from the British Library.

ISBN 978-0-7499-2507-9

Edited by Krystyna Mayer
Design and make up by Paul Saunders
Illustrations by Rodney Paull

Printed and bound in Great Britain by
MPG Books, Bodmin, Cornwall

Piatkus
An imprint of
Little, Brown Book Group
100 Victoria Embankment
London EC4Y 0DY

An Hachette UK Company
www.hachette.co.uk

www.piatkus.co.uk

Dedication

This book is dedicated to my parents Bill and Rita Nelson,
who in their wisdom encouraged me to find my own
spiritual path, opening me to an inner understanding
of my connection to Spirit.

MARY NELSON

… and for me, this one's for Debbie Thomas, whose unerring
management, administration and LaStone talent have allowed
me the freedom to develop, expand, and generally go off and do
my own thing – confident that everything is in safe and
professional hands. Thank you.

JANE SCRIVNER

Contents

Foreword by Mary Nelson

It is my pleasure to introduce Jane Scrivner's book on LaStone therapy.

I first became aware of the use of stones and their healing qualities in the summer of 1993, and I began to share this ancient knowledge with other body-workers. In 1998, after taking one of my workshops, Jane began an intense study programme with me, which led to her becoming a certified LaStone instructor the following year.

As time went on, Jane and I spoke about the history of the stones, their magic healing properties, and how best we might share all of this with the general public. In these pages Jane shares the secrets of the ancient medicine of stone healing, blending its magic with LaStone's history. She has elegantly interwoven the strands of my own personal story – which will, I hope, open your heart and mind to a fuller understanding of the relationship that has existed between humans and stones since time began.

It is my hope that through Jane's enchanting book you will enjoy exploring the stones' story as much as we did.

MARY NELSON
April 2004

Foreword by Jane Scrivner

This handbook sets out to be a detailed factual and practical guide to becoming a LaStone therapist. It details the original treatment – the treatment and technique that were channelled to Mary Nelson in 1993. In fact the manuscript for the manual was completed ten years to the month from when the treatment began, in August 1993.

The LaStone therapy Original Body course teaches the basics and principles of the original treatment that Mary Nelson began in 1993. This treatment has developed and evolved though learning and experience. You will also develop and evolve as a LaStone therapist and we totally encourage that – but first you need to learn the basics of the treatment.

You may wish to think of the LaStone Original Body course as your climbing frame to your future as a therapist. The course aims to get you where you want to be using the principles of LaStone in a safe and structured way. When you have the foundations you can build upon them; without them you may not be on such safe ground. Once you have studied the Original Body course there are many ways to enhance your knowledge, and these are described in detail further on in this section.

Studying the LaStone handbook is a great way to start your stone journey; you will not be disappointed, only challenged and enlightened.

The handbook has been an ongoing project since the treatment began. Many people have been involved in it and it has appeared in numerous versions. This is the first-ever published handbook, and it is a collaboration between myself and Mary Nelson and all the people acknowledged below. Our heartfelt thanks to all of you.

JANE SCRIVNER

Acknowledgements from Mary Nelson

This book is a result of my ongoing teaching of LaStone therapy to the many massage therapists who have sought the knowledge of Mother Earth revealed through the benefits of heated and cold stones. The eagerness of other body-workers to know more, and to have a reference manual, has inspired this book. I thank each student who encouraged me to finish the book – not only for their own personal use, but to honour my teaching of LaStone therapy. I take pleasure in each of you who honour the stones, and call this treatment LaStone therapy.

LaStone therapy is the name San Juanette channelled to me in the spring of 1994. San Juanette is one of my spiritual guides who directs me in the use of the Stone People. 'Pick up the stones and use them,' was the first message I received. Over the years I have been receiving many more messages and directions on how to use the stones. I am delighted that I was chosen to learn and teach this form of healing, using the stones. Thank you San Juanette, the Stone People and Mother Earth for showing me a way to bring balance back into our daily lives by using the electromagnetic energy that exists in all things.

My heartfelt thanks to my dear friends, who in their own way contributed to the making of this book: to William Myers, Valerie Sorrells, Tenanche Semiata-Akuaba and Bob Akuaba for the many hours spent talking about Mother Earth, and the variables of energy work treatments; to Tomi Wertheim for her endless help with this book and the company LST; to Mary Casebeer for helping to edit this manual in its early stages – thank you dear Mary. Thank you to Patricia Warne, for her priceless advice and explanations of thermotherapy and the principle of application of hot and cold stones to the body. To Teena Pleshek for her ability to endure all the changes I made as this book continued to grow and develop, and for the long hours she has spent adjusting the pages of my corrections.

I would like to express my gratitude to Betsy Grace Sandlin for her ability to see what my goal was in this book and her painless and loving way of editing in the early years of the book's development. In 1999 Teena Pleshek, one of our senior instructors, expressed her desire to assist me in restructuring the book; that was the beginning of what you now hold in your hands. I am especially grateful for the hours Teena has put into the making of this book.

With deep appreciation, I wish to thank Janette Grell-Morin for her lovely drawings, which gave life to the pages in earlier versions of this book. It is with great honour that Jo Schmitz agreed to photograph the stones for me. Her keen eye for placement enhanced every shot.

I thank my two children, Henry and Rita, who have allowed me to occupy our computer, taking up precious hours of game time, and for all their pats on my back as they pass by, saying, 'How you doing, Mum?'

I would like to thank my loving father, who has always been there for me. He not only gifted me with my first computer, but also came by regularly and backed up my records, just in case.

Special thanks go to Bill Updegrove and his colleagues at the University of Arizona for their many hours of research into and discussions about the type of basalt stone that was chosen for LaStone therapy.

I will be forever grateful to the staff of Kinko's on Broadway and Craycroft in Tucson, Arizona; for the countless hours they have spent in printing and binding hundreds of LaStone therapy books for my workshops before we were blessed with this, our first published version. Without their guardianship and interest this would have been an unbearable task. I was most pleased that the printing of my book was in the caring hands of Greg Berven and his staff at Postal Annex in Menasha, Wisconsin.

Special thanks go to my niece Tonya Council-Bucinell for allowing me to use the stones on her that very first day when the messages began to come to me from Spirit. And thanks to all my clients now and at the beginning, for their willingness to experience each new method as it came to me, and for the wonderful feedback I received about each technique as I experimented on them one by one.

Most importantly I extend my loving appreciation to Spirit for being by my side every step of my life and awakening my inner teacher. To Mother Earth and all she has to offer and to the Stone Clan People for speaking to me on that summer day. To The Great Mystery, The Creator, because I exist and so does the entire universe.

I hope that all students of LaStone go on to experience even just a little of the riches I have received from my relationship with the Stone Clan People, the Ancient Ones.

Course Descriptions

As previously mentioned, this handbook details the Original Body course, which is the course based on the channelled information Mary Nelson received in summer of 1993. Many more courses have become available due to our explorations of the potential of the stones and interpretations of their messages.

Your current qualification will probably determine which course you choose as a starting point for your own personal journey with the stones, but we encourage you to look at the many different ways of enhancing your knowledge and to develop and refresh your own ability to work with the stones.

Each course can be used towards **Continuing Education Units (CEUs)** in the US and we are working towards the same recognition in all countries that have a similar 'continuing education' system. Please speak with your instructor or contact LaStone for the most up-to-date information.

The following levels are used in recognition of further study:

- LST (LaStone Therapist): completion of one LaStone workshop.

- ALST (Advanced LaStone Therapist): completion of four LaStone workshops.

- MLST (Master LaStone Therapist): completion of seven LaStone workshops.

Original Body

Original Body may well be your first journey, involving exploring the use of alternating temperatures and energy work within a massage session. This course focuses on the foundation and beginnings of LaStone therapy in modern times. Here you will learn the fundamentals of geothermotherapy and the art of balance and relaxation for you and your clients using simple yet effective energy techniques.

Once you have started your journey there are many options; LaStone are constantly updating the training, fine tuning the facts and adding new dimensions. As a result the courses open to you are also constantly changing. The details of the most recent courses are always posted on our website, www.lastonetherapy.com, and they include advanced, master and many other levels of training.

This handbook introduces you to the first steps of your training; where they take you is up to you and your imagination.

CHAPTER 1

What is LaStone Therapy?

KEY POINTS

- LaStone therapy was originated in 1993 by Mary Nelson, in Tucson, Arizona, the United States.

- LaStone therapy uses stones for work on the body and also for placement under and on the body during the treatment.

- LaStone therapy delivers the principles of geothermotherapy – alternating the application of heated and chilled stones – to the body.

- LaStone therapy reflects and aims to create balance and harmony on all levels.

- LaStone therapy uses deep, penetrating massage techniques and highly effective energy work.

- LaStone therapy effects chemical, physical and spiritual healing within the mind, body and spirit.

- LaStone therapy has roots in Native American traditions and beliefs.

- LaStone therapy will prolong the life of the therapist in terms of physical injury prevention and emotional and spiritual protection.

- The LaStone treatment is totally flexible; once a therapist has studied Original Body they will know how to add LaStone to any treatment they are qualified to do.

General Information

LaStone therapy has many levels. It has a huge spectrum of ability and a huge spectrum of possibility. Wherever you are as a therapist, there is a perfect place for you to start on your stone journey. As on any journey, you will be challenged; you will trip up, discover and see some amazing things and have some extraordinary experiences, and you will develop your own personal abilities.

LaStone is about balance – creating and maintaining balance. If you are currently very physical as a therapist we will challenge your ideas, enabling you to become more emotional and spiritual. If you are currently working on a spiritual or energetic level we can show you the physical and chemical changes you can effect. Rest assured that you will see how the stones will balance out your current way of thinking and working.

We will work with the physical, emotional and spiritual; with the heated and chilled; through pain and release. We will challenge our clients on all levels of their being. You will see how temperature can challenge and create balance, how you can awaken your clients to their own spirituality, and how you can remove age-old pain and discomfort and return to health – all through the use of the stones. The balance will become obvious: black and white, heated and chilled, Yin and Yang, male and female, above and below, Sun and Moon. Very soon you will understand the perfect sense this treatment makes.

So how to answer the question 'What is LaStone therapy?'

You will find your answer once you have completed the course. You will find a way to describe what you will do with the stones and how your own personal treatment develops. We are not going to give you a standard response because there is no standard treatment. It is for you to decide what you are comfortable with, what you are doing within your LaStone treatment and what your client will hear. All responses to the question are right, as long as you honour the stones. If you do this, then however you describe your treatment the stones will work for you.

If you are a remedial or sports therapist focusing on the phenomenal ability of the alternating temperatures to effect internal chemical change, the stones will still be sorting the emotional and spiritual side for you. If you work with energy and spiritual healing, rest assured that the heated and chilled temperatures will still be balancing the physical body. Mind, body and spirit are inseparable. The stones know this and no matter how you describe them they still do their job.

LaStone therapy uses heated and frozen stones to deliver the deeply therapeutic, relaxing, grounding, deep-tissue and cleansing treatment. The principles of thermotherapy, geothermotherapy, deep-tissue manipulation, auric field work, chakra response and spirituality are all used in perfect combination. The name LaStone therapy can in fact be reworked to say 'last one therapy' – the last word in therapy.

LaStone is a journey that can begin with the energy work and spiritual awakenings that are experienced with the aura and placement sequences – this way it is suited to the healing and more holistic client and therapist. Alternatively it can be approached with the chemical and physical change of the body and structures that come about as a result of the thermotherapy – in this case it is ideally suited to the sports and remedial therapist and the client wanting deeper work. All that said, here is some help from Mary Nelson if you still need it.

Clinically it is the application of geothermotherapy, using deep, penetrating heated stones and alternating with chilled stones to bring about a chemical release within the body's systems, to balance and recharge our souls with Mother Earth and the Father Sky as we each perceive their wonder. Using different temperatures, heated or chilled, on the body to bring about a certain reaction has been done for eons. Adjusting temperatures in bodywork to aid clients in healing has always been beneficial.

In Orignal Body, I will show you a way to use these different temperatures in conjunction with Mother Earth and the Stone People to bring about balance and healing in your clients. Bring Mother Earth and the stones' energies into the treatment and let them do the walking along the muscles, allowing your client to reconnect to the inner strength of Mother Earth.

Remember what it was like as a child to lie upon the Earth and feel as though nothing was wrong in your life? People are searching far and wide for that sense of well-being, that connection with the power and peace of life. We have forgotten where to find it. In this fast-paced society that we live in, we rarely take time to go outdoors and rest and feel the vibration of our mother, the Earth. It is too convenient to go to the gym; some of us even have workout equipment at home. We are missing the true meaning of why one goes outside, not realising that we need the connection to Mother Earth as much as we need to exercise. This is why LaStone therapy is so popular. The vibrations and temperatures of the stones remind us of our connection to Mother Earth, supporting us in feeling cradled and protected.

Mary Nelson, Founder

Here is further information from Patricia Warne, who is the geothermotherapy advisor for LaStone Therapy Inc.

A contemporary approach to alternating temperatures in massage, LaStone therapy is a multi-faceted technique designed to benefit client and therapist at once. The therapeutic potential of this treatment goes beyond measure. The physiological benefits of alternating temperatures to the body have long been scientifically and medically proven. LaStone therapy capitalises on these traditional practices with a current approach.

The different stones are the medium and the alternating temperatures are the message. This 'vascular gymnastic' of the circulatory system assists the body in self-healing. LaStone therapy administers this principle with unerring elegance. Therapists discover that the stress and strain to their hands, wrists and arms are virtually eliminated by using our technique. The stones and thermal variation do all the heavy work for them. They are able to work more efficiently for longer periods of time.

All of those involved in this training will develop more reverence for daily work and rituals, because respect and appreciation grow naturally from this fertile learning experience. LaStone therapy produces alternately sedative and re-energising responses in the body. Clients love the potent recharge they receive during the treatment. As they walk into the sacred stream of life, they unanimously express the same words as they leave the treatment table: 'I feel blessed, balanced and cradled by Mother Earth.' They smile and turn confidently towards the day ahead.

LaStone therapy goes beyond the physical experience of typical massage, and enters deeper dimensions of relaxation, health and well-being, creating a positive approach to body-mind-spirit philosophy. Not only is this an advancement in therapeutic massage and the true meaning of body-mind-soul techniques for your clients' benefit; it is also an absolute solution to the strain and injuries to our wrists and thumbs that we, as massage therapists, experience daily. Using LaStone therapy on each of your clients will eliminate strain to your thumbs, and will help to maintain healthy wrists by preventing hyperflexion and hyper-extension. Learn to let the stones do the heavy work for you. Give your thumbs and wrists a long-deserved rest. Mastering the art of LaStone therapy will not only increase your clientele, but also add many years to your career as a massage therapist.

For me LaStone therapy is the means by which I can aid a client to balance all levels of emotional, mental, physical and spiritual energies, and often unlock blocked memories, to facilitate remembrance of where they came from and who they are in this Spiritual Universe.

Patricia Warne, Geothermotherapy expert and advisor

EXERCISE

Write a paragraph that explains LaStone therapy to your clients in concise but informative way. Try to include all the important factual information as well as describing the physical and spiritual experience. Revisit this paragraph every six months to see how you can revise it in line with the growth of your own experiences with the stones.

Well done – this is your first marketing tool.

The Origins of LaStone Therapy

KEY POINTS

- LaStone therapy started in the summer of 1993.

- At this time, Mary Nelson was looking for a way to protect and heal her already damaged and aching limbs. The damage had been caused by overwork in her very successful massage clinic. LaStone became the solution.

- LaStone was channelled to Mary Nelson by her Native American spirit guide called San Juanette.

- The name LaStone came about through prayer and guidance with San Juanette.

- The treatment came about through a combination of prayer, experimentation and inspiration.

- The original treatment came about in a few weeks but the learning never stops!

The Story and the Facts

When Mary Nelson received LaStone therapy, she didn't know who she had received it from or why, and it didn't even have a name. She had simply asked for help.

If you were asked to design a treatment, you would take what you know, choose the best bits and put them together in a format that you knew from experience was different, effective and interesting. If you were asked to explain your new treatment, you would be able to break it down, element by element, and describe the value and purpose of each stage. You might include experiences and anecdotes, but you would definitely know about every aspect of your new therapy – the history and the detail.

In the case of LaStone therapy, the treatment came first, and we will never stop the studying that constantly reveals how effective and powerful it is. You will discover some amazing things yourself on your Original Body course, as will your fellow therapists and all your clients.

From the moment the treatment was channelled to Mary she has been working to answer the whats and the whys. This process will never end. The treatment came first and we can now spend the rest of our lives filling in the reasons, the techniques, the theory, the reality and the spirituality. The treatment develops every day through experience and the learning will never stop.

LaStone has only just begun and we will never fully understand its full potential. Any time, money and knowledge we have is being injected into the study of LaStone therapy. The courses will develop as the learning grows. The stones are being constantly made by Mother Earth and as long as she is producing things we will use her tools to learn.

The Power of Ten

This treatment came about to protect future therapists; to help them physically and emotionally to work deeper and more effectively with no damage to themselves.

We believe that one stroke with a stone is worth ten with your hands – the treatment is ten times deeper for ten times less effort. It lasts ten times longer than traditional techniques. As a therapist you will be able to work for ten years longer and increase your practice ten-fold. Just think the power of ten!

From Mary Nelson:

Receiving the Stones

LaStone therapy came to me in the summer of 1993, while my niece Tonya Council-Bucinell and I were sitting in a sauna room that was not working up to standard at the time. We were staring at the hot rocks that were warming the wooden decks we were resting on. I was struggling with a recurring shoulder injury and needed some type of extra help when working on trigger points in my clients. I silently asked Spirit for answers to why I was in so much pain and how was I to do massages with this shoulder. The first message I received from Spirit was, 'Use the stones.' Use them for what? was my first thought. Then my mind went back to the pain in my shoulder, and I wondered how was I going to massage Tonya, who was in my office for a treatment. Her complaint for the day was a blockage in both rhomboids; with my sports massage training I knew this meant she needed deep-tissue techniques in this area. I worried about causing myself more debilitating pain.

Again the voice said, 'Use the stones.' I listened a little, but took no action. As we were leaving to go and do the massage, the voice called out louder, 'Pick up the stones and use them.' How could I ignore that voice? It was loud and clear as to what Spirit wanted. I chose two palm-sized stones and dropped them into a pot of ginger fomentation that I had prepared earlier that morning to use on Tonya. I found that mild pressure with the warm stone was enough to release her tense rhomboid muscles. The heat and weight of the small stones did it all, saving me painful extra effort, and this allowed my shoulder to rest and heal. Before the treatment was complete with Tonya, I went back to the sauna room and retrieved a few more stones, dropping them in the hot ginger water; I applied a few more warm stones on Tonya. She just loved the results and was very pleased with this new-found toy I had acquired while she and I had sat in the broken sauna room. After the treatment with Tonya I went back to the sauna room and retrieved six or seven more smooth stones from the bed of rocks resting in their wooden home. I had three more clients to practise on with my new friends; I was so excited and full of energy and renewed excitement about doing bodywork.

By the end of the week I had collected every single smooth stone from the wooden box in the sauna room, and had about thirty-six to forty stones. I had called every single place selling rocks in Tucson and visited most of them, looking for more of the same stone, because I needed to return the stones to the sauna room before it was repaired. This type of stone was very hard to come by and the stones you could buy for sauna beds were not smooth but rough and pointy; they just would not do for massage. I did purchase a large box of these stones to replace the smooth ones I had borrowed during this first week. The sauna room had not yet been repaired by the time the stones arrived, so these new stones just rested in their wooden home not knowing what they were there for. About two months went by before they were charged with heat to offer life and warmth to the clients of the Athletic Club.

It was within that first week that I placed stones in the freezer to chill them; working in an athletic club much of my massage practice involved using cryotherapy on injuries and over-worked muscles incurred by athletes. I discovered quickly that some stones did not hold the heat as well as others, so these stones were placed in a small ice chest and that was then placed in the walk-in freezer in the restaurant of the club. I loved working with the chilled stones instead of ice; they did not melt and that was a big plus for both the clients and myself.

As my clients began to report that their bodies felt as though they had changed, and that they experienced a feeling of well-being after a treatment with the stones, I started to long to have the stones placed on my body, to feel their healing powers work their magic on me as well. So I began to take time every night after I was done for the day to lie with the stones. I practised doing layouts on my body similar to the ones we now do when we build castles of stones on each other during the first day of the Original Body workshop. As I would rest with the warm and cool stones on my body, images of stones on clients' bodies would appear to me deep within the third eye area of my head. This was fascinating to me – it was energising and revealing as to what Spirit wanted from the stones and myself.

As I continued to rest with the stones each night and to work on myself, more messages began to come through even faster than when I was working with the stones in my hands on a client. With each day's work, I was intuitively led to use more stones, and developed a method of progressively opening up the energy channels of the body. I was also working more deeply into the muscles with each application of a warm stone and offering chilled stones in areas of injury and inflammation. In the early days I was very conservative when it came to applying chilled stones to the body. In my education and study of sports massage, we were taught to only apply ice to an area of inflammation and injury. I kept with this philosophy for about three years, until we began to experiment with how the body responds to the Yin and nurturing energy aspects of a chilled stone, the colour white and the marble itself. We now of course use chilled stones for many reasons during a LaStone treatment.

The following story is one that only a few people have heard to date. It is a very private experience for me and one that I hope offers you insight into how I became aware of who I am in this universe. I share this story with you in the hope that you too can find your inner teacher through self-awareness, prayer and meditation.

As I began to grow with the stones I longed to know the voice that continued to speak to me from deep within my heart. I asked Spirit to guide me and knew without doubt that I would be shown how to find this Spirit that speaks to me. As I prepared my body with the stones one night, I asked for this to be made clear to me. As soon as I placed the last stone on my third eye, I drifted off, out of body, not aware of time or space.

I found my body lying on a dirt floor in a very small room; it was dark outside and the only light coming into the room was from the moon. There in the room with me was a young man and an older woman. The woman seemed to be doing some form of healing work on my body – it appeared that there was bleeding from my chest cavity. It was odd to me to be in the state of pure energy and to be watching this event before me. The young man seemed to be very distressed about the fact that I was dying.

As I lay there I saw who I was – a young maiden who had not yet reached adult-hood, who was on a medicine path of study with this elder who was attending me. I had no worries, no regrets; no sorrow was present within my being. As I stood there observing my body take its last breath, I watched the young man as he came to terms with my body passing into the light, and saw how the wise woman held space and time for this moment to finalise in reality.

Watching these three people act out this whole experience, I realised that I was not only the young woman on the floor passing into the light. I was also the young man finding his way as he lost control over a situation, and the wise woman holding space as the events were allowed to unfold while Great Mystery's plan came to fruition. It was at that moment that I saw the young woman, the young man and the wise woman as the voice that speaks to me about the stones. At that moment I fully comprehended that my inner teacher was a combination of these souls' energies coming through me with gifts from the heavens and times past. It became clear to me that as souls, we travel through time and space as individuals and yet joined with each other for a common purpose; that at any one moment in time we may be a combination of multiple souls' energies, offering insight and guidance while walking the path of a Human Being with honour and respect for all life and the Great Mystery that surrounds us and engulfs us as one.

As this enlightenment came to me I took in a deep breath and awoke from my dream state with a renewal of life and an awareness of what my path is at this time on the planet. Realising that I hold within my field of energy three souls that speak to me as one, I again wanted to know more. As I began to clean up the stones and build a mosaic with them on the massage table to show honour and respect for the gift of insight they had just shared with me, I asked to have the voice of this Spirit be known to me.

When I awoke at around 3 a.m., I went to my computer. This is something I often do – in fact most of this book was written at around that time of the morning. I seem to listen to Spirit best in the early morning hours, when life is still in my house and the phone isn't ringing and the children aren't in need of my attention. As I sat there with my fingers on the keys, I began to type letters, and the voice said, 'No that's not it.' Again, letters found their way to the screen; I heard 'No that's not it' again and again, until I finally heard the voice said, 'Yes, that is my name.' The name on the screen was San Juanette. I was not sure how to pronounce this name, so I repeated the name over and over again until I heard, 'That's it' when I said 'San Wa ney'. I was then satisfied with the answer Spirit blessed me with on that early September morning.

The Name LaStone

I first called this form of bodywork Hot Stone Massage (along with many variations of that). In a very short time, however, I began to incorporate chilled stones into my work. No longer was the name Hot Stone Massage complementary to what I was accomplishing in my work with my clients. I again went to bed and asked for guidance from San Juanette. I asked, 'What do you want to call this that I am doing with the stones?' When three o'clock rolled around, my sleep was again disturbed. As I got out of bed I heard the words la stone therapy. 'Now how do I spell that one?' was my thought.

Mary typed the words as she thought they should be written and the computer kept throwing back the words 'listen' or 'last one', both of which are extremely relevant. LaStone is the 'last one therapy' or 'the last word in therapy', the ultimate therapy. We should also learn to 'listen' to the lessons the stones have for us – either as therapists or clients.

EXERCISE

Write a nine-sentence story about the origins of LaStone therapy. Use the key points at the start of this chapter (*see page 6*) to focus on the most important and descriptive parts of this amazing story.

CHAPTER 3

LaStone Therapy – the History

KEY POINTS

- LaStone therapy – the Original Stone massage using heated and chilled stones.

- There is nothing new in LaStone; its components have their own ancient history.

- Massage is thousands of years old.

- The stones are millions of years old; we are not the first to use them in treatment.

- Thermotherapy is thousands of years old; we are not the first to use the chemical changes the stones manifest.

- Energy has been with us since before the Earth was formed; energy shift created this planet we live on.

- Mother Nature and Father Sky have been providing since we began.

- This is no gimmick – LaStone is here to stay and will form the bedrock(!) of all future therapies.

- LaStone is creating its own history and we are a part of it.

- We now have many other companies and therapists using other expressions of stone work in their practices. Copying is the sincerest form of flattery – we take it as a compliment, knowing that LaStone is the Original Stone massage treatment.

The History

- There is nothing new in LaStone therapy:

- Stones have been around as long as the Earth has.

- Hot and cold have been used in alternation for ages.

- The stones used are millions of years old.

- Everyone knows about massage . . .

Although LaStone therapy may be one of the newest treatments available, it is grounded in some of the oldest, most valuable, most tried and tested therapies known to man. It is at once the newest, most advanced natural treatment available, and the oldest, most valuable and profound therapy you can have. To learn from the stones is to study under the oldest and wisest teachers.

LaStone therapy is the ultimate dichotomy, involving the furthest of extremes: heated and chilled, basalt and marble (and many other stones), Sun and Moon, male and female, Yin and Yang, black and white, relaxing and invigorating, sedative and euphoric, active and passive, vasodilation and vasoconstriction, Mother Earth and Father Sky.

The Stones

Stones have been used in ceremonies and treatments that are as old as the Incas, the Shang Dynasty in China of around 1500 BC and the ancient Egyptian pyramids.

We now know that the oldest rocks on Earth actually came from outer space in the form of meteorites. This stone type is called chondrite, and the earliest pieces can be dated to as far back as 4,600 million years ago. It wasn't until much later that rocks actually began to form on the Earth – some 4,200 million years ago (mere youngsters!). Native Americans have respected the Stone Clan People since their time began. Using them for worship, guidance and healing they know them and respect them as the Ancient Ones.

Stones have been used in healing for many ages, but what about the other aspects of this treatment?

Thermotherapy and Geothermotherapy

The alternate application of heated and chilled temperatures, known as thermotherapy, was documented as early as the eighteenth century, but it is believed that the use of hot and cold bathing was an integral part of Hippocratic beliefs – and Hippocrates died *c*. 430 BC.

Sebastian Kneipp, a German living in the nineteenth century, was a great believer in the power and therapeutic qualities of water. He believed that the free flow of blood and circulation in our bodies was the secret of total health and well-being. Kneipp was one of the first practitioners to use the alternating temperatures of water to boost the body's circulation in order to achieve optimum health.

It is to Kneipp that we owe the sitz bath, which involves bathing in cool and heated water. Indeed, the practice of taking a cold shower in the morning can be traced back to Kneipp and his efforts to improve our circulation and boost our immunity from right at the beginning of the day.

Today, we are very familiar with spas but they are actually nothing new. We may think that spa use is undergoing a huge boost as something new and exciting, but spas have been around for a long time. They were originally used to improve health and well-being – and not just as a luxury method of relaxation as they are today. Spas were about getting better, and the hot pools, cold dips, plunge pools, saunas and steam rooms were designed to balance the body so that it could heal.

The same principles apply in LaStone – we use alternating temperatures to heal. The term geothermotherapy is used because the Earth (*geo*) is used to deliver the temperature, through the stones.

Massage

Massage too can be traced back to Greek and Roman physicians. Hippocrates wrote: 'The physician must be experienced in many things, but assuredly in rubbing … for rubbing can bind a joint that is too loose, and loosen a joint that is too rigid'. Hopefully we have moved on a little from basic 'rubbing', but the principles still apply.

Energy Work

Energy and healing work is an integral part of many ancient cultures. The Chinese have Chi or Qi, the Japanese Ki, Indians work with Prana and Reiki practitioners use the influence of the Universal Life Force. We have meridians, auric fields and chakras. We work with crystals and vibrations, use guides and spirits, and can work with much, much more. Almost every indigenous tribe, culture and group has a belief structure that can be incorporated into the treatment. The respect for the individual is never compromised – simply balanced and healed.

Mother Earth and Father Sky

Nature is the strongest element we have on Earth. The planet came about as a result of nature's forces working together. As humans we tend to think we are in charge. We are not, and every now and then Mother Nature and Father Sky decide to remind us of their strengths and we are put in our place very quickly. A little too much rain and we have floods; a little too much sun and we get droughts. We plant plants and have them grow, but the plants we concentrate on the most – the weeds – are the ones that return time after time despite the fact that we keep hacking them back and ripping them out. These are the plants that nature put there, and they will never go away. Everything we use today comes from the earth or sky. Metal, fabrics, drinking water, paper – all these and more come from nature.

LaStone therapy respects nature and uses its strengths to make the treatment the most wonderful and healing therapy that there is.

So who else has realised how valuable stones are? Since the dawn of time, people have been drawn to the energies of the stones. You only have to look around to see the traces of this that we have left from centuries of walking on Mother Earth. We have carried monstrous stones unspeakable distances, to honour kings and gods. We have created monuments of stones, and carved our own faces and those of our gods on stones. There exist many stone reminders of mysterious or forgotten people, for instance the statues on Easter Island, the Egyptian sphinx and pyramids, the Inca temples, Machu Picchu and Stonehenge. Of more recent origin, there is Mount Rushmore in North America.

Lava stones and basalt stone were used for building altars for religious or magical practices. The Incas coated theirs in gold and constructed sun and moon temples for worship. In 2000 on a visit to Peru I saw with my own eyes just how revered this stone was and realised that it had been carried over phenomenal distances. The enormous sizes of stone the Incas worked with are almost impossible to imagine. The fact that there were no lengths they wouldn't go to in order to build stone temples for worship was very evident in every religious, respected or valued place we saw.

Then there are the worry stones people carry in their pockets; and stone fetishes are created for many forms of healing, rebirth, wealth and relationships.

As part of their deep respect for stones, Native Americans use heated stones in their sweat lodges, usually the bluish-to-black stones. In the Native American Sioux tradition, a boy going through manhood would lie on a hard rock and put smooth stones between his toes to learn the difference between hard and soft, female and male. He would thus gain a beginning of an understanding of how important it is to balance one's life. Maybe we could introduce this technique into primary school lesson plans!

Many shamans, medicine people and spiritual healers all over the world use stones and crystals in their healing ceremonies. Each colour and type of stone reflects energy and a purpose, and a clearing and releasing effect on the client as it is being used. Very few people are chosen to learn from a spiritual teacher how to use the stones for healing. A shaman will usually pass on the knowledge of healing to one special student before passing into the Light to rejoin the creator. This is one reason why there is very little information available for research purposes. Here are some examples of how stones were and sometimes still are used for healing and soothing purposes around the world.

- The healing women of the Mapuche tribes in Chile used black stones in their healing work and for divination.

- In Hawaii the Kahunas use lava stones in their healing treatments, and they wrap the stone in a ki (ti) leaf. The lava stone represents healing and protection.

- In the Philippines it is a common practice to use a rough basalt stone, which we know as pumice, to slough off old and dry skin. Many women today still use these porous pumice stones in the bath to maintain smooth, silky skin. Pumice is in fact the only type of stone that floats!

- In Russia there is a tradition of using heated black stones in the bath. People line the bottoms of their bathtubs with hot, smooth stones and then lie down on them, soaking in the soothing warm energy that radiates from each stone.

- In the days when cowboys roamed the American countryside, it was common practice for them to heat stones in the fire and then place them on the ground under their bedding. The stones' heated energies not only kept them warm at night, but the stones were also more giving to the body than the earth for comfort.

- The Japanese people may use smooth black stones to keep their abdomens warm after a meal. It is a custom of theirs not to eat a lot at one time, so traditionally they sometimes place two or three warm stones in the sash that is wrapped around their waist, which gives them a sense of being fuller for a longer period of time.

- The Mayan Indians use a divination stone to tell them what illness a person has, and what the treatment(s) should be to aid them back to good health.

- In China the use of heated stones to relieve tired muscles dates back to before the Shang Dynasty (*c.* 2000–1500 BC).

- Native Americans sometimes use a sun-heated (heliotherapy) stone on the belly of a woman when her menses are painful, to relieve the pain.

Modern-day Stone Therapy

As is the case with anything that is good, there will be groups bringing out similar versions that use the same techniques, and try to improve them or emulate them. This is extremely flattering and it is now possible to see many different types of stone therapy on the market.

LaStone therapy was and is the original stone therapy in the modern day. It is Mary Nelson's channelled message and her experience, experimentation and wisdom that has given us the LaStone treatment we know today.

Still, therapists do sometimes worry. Are the treatments as good as other stone therapies? Are they better? Are they worse? Is there a practice in my area? Is there anyone in competition? I don't want to tread on anyone's toes . . .

Our advice is to chill. If your concern as a therapist is that you may lose

business to these other companies or therapists, then just make sure you practise, honour the stones and yourself and see what manifests. If you stay small
and secret so that you don't show your skills and don't give anything away, then
– according to the laws of Karma (the Sanskrit for comeback) – you will get
nothing in return. According to the same principle, if you give out negativity
and fear they will come back on you – usually when you least expect it. If, however, you give out skill, good intentions and healing the results should be
extremely rewarding for you.

EXERCISE

Review this chapter and commit to memory three ways in which the
stones have been used in history, three ways we use thermotherapy in
day-to-day life, and three examples of how powerful Mother Nature and
Father Sky can be.

Mary Nelson – the Founder of LaStone Therapy

KEY POINTS

- Mary Dolores Nelson was born in Tucson, Arizona, the United States on 14 September 1954.

- She originated LaStone Therapy in August 1993.

- She created LaStone Therapy Inc.

- She continues to practise and teach LaStone Therapy.

Briefly . . .

Mary Nelson is a mother of two; she is extremely spiritual and down to earth, and a bit of a LaStone guru. She works really hard to keep the LaStone message out there.

In More Detail . . .

Mary Nelson was the middle child of five children, an older brother and sister and two younger brothers. She was raised in an Irish Catholic family that held true to the Irish Catholic traditions. Christ and God were ever present in her upbringing. Coming from Irish origins, there were always nuns and priests visiting her home, and telling stories and bringing gifts that enriched and confirmed her beliefs. As a young woman, Mary began to study metaphysical beliefs in addition to maintaining her Catholic faith. This sometimes caused problems and Mary would often stay 'quiet' rather than risk the wrath of her concerned family.

For twenty-eight years, Mary chose not to speak about what she saw or heard from her guides. In those days even though she did not know for sure who they were, she gave them names associating them with Christian saints and angels. Then a time came in her late thirties when she saw them more as spirit guides than as saints. Mary's ability to combine her metaphysical experiences with her Catholic beliefs without compromising either also enabled her to study Native American cultures. This brought about her ability to remain spiritually, energetically and physically 'in touch' in her life and was probably the key to her being able to receive the teachings of the stones from her spirit guide.

Mary left school wanting to become a vet, but was unable to take the course. Instead, she studied interior design and dress design in college. Some time after this she found herself managing a health store in Tucson, Arizona. At the same time she undertook a massage course at the now-famous Desert Institute for Healing Arts in Arizona, and graduated with honours. The course opened up a whole new world of energy work, not just through the actual study, but also because of her intuitive need to do more than just follow the 'stroke sheets'.

During her training, Mary started to develop some of the techniques for her massage practice that have now become fundamental to the LaStone therapy treatment we know today. 'Opening and Closing Spiral', 'Spinal Spiral' and 'Up the Left and Down the Right' have all become mantras in the LaStone courses. The terminology may not be familiar to energy workers but the research Mary has subsequently done and the sharing of these experiences has shown us that they have origins that are nearly as old as the stones themselves.

After qualifying Mary went on to practise massage and very soon built a strong and successful practice. The practice did so well that, like many therapists, she began to feel the strain that comes with working on other people every day of the week. No matter how anatomically correct you try to be, there will always be damage to the muscles you need to use so intensively while you are practising massage. Any therapist reading this book will know only too well the feeling of aching joints and potential damage to fingers and thumbs that comes with repeated use. As a therapist Mary found this difficult to cope with – the desire to do the best work possible for her clients combined with the pain she felt after just a few treatments, with many more bookings to fulfil before each day was over.

The situation began to change in August 1993. On 19 August 1993 Mary listened to her inner teacher when she spoke to her about the stones and how to use them. At the time, she had an injury to her right shoulder that caused a lot of pain, and she needed a method that would be easier on her and beneficial to her clients. She knew she needed help and therefore asked for it. The rest, as they say, is history, which is described in fabulous detail in *LaStone Therapy* (*see* Further Resources, *page 184*).

EXERCISE

Study the full history of LaStone therapy. Read *LaStone Therapy* (Piatkus Books).

The Stones

KEY POINTS

- Trust your stones – they are there to help you.

- Don't worry about getting to know your stones – you *will* get to know them.

- Your stones will become so familiar to you that you will eventually have a favourite stone for almost every stroke you do.

- Spend time getting to know the stones.

- With the exception of a few stones, every stone has a partner. This makes the strokes feel balanced, just as your hands do.

- If you are not sure of a pair of stones, close your eyes and hold the two stones – do they *feel* equal?

- You must care for your stones every time they are used (*see page 54*).

- The way we show you how to use the stones will be the most effective way in 99 per cent of your treatments. You will, however, need to make decisions on the stone used depending on the stroke you want to do, the size of your clients, their health, their muscle condition, and so on.

- Wherever you use a hot stone, you will have a cool alternative.

- Fifty-four heated stones are used for the heated application.

- A minimum of eighteen stones are used for the chilled application.

- One Chinese fluorite or selenite wand can be used for spinal spirals.

- One labradorite stone is used to recharge all the stones.

- One petoskey stone is used for the third eye stone. .

- The heated and chilled stones are developing all the time. We currently use eight different types: basalt, jade, marble, sardonyx, onyx and petoskey are just some of the varieties.

Before we even start discussing the stone sets, there a few things worth mentioning. Together with the energy work, the stones are the most important part of the LaStone treatment. If you know the history and theory behind the treatment, you can be extremely informative, *but* if you don't know your stones, stone technique and the energy work, you are not going to be the best LaStone therapist you can be.

Getting to know your stones takes time, so don't go off in a tailspin because you don't get it perfect the first time you prepare your set. You will eventually get to know the stones so well that you will be able to sort them in moments – even while you are talking to people and dealing with other things; this *will* become second nature. So just chill and enjoy getting to know your new work-pals.

Think of this: when you started school, there were probably upwards of twenty people in your class. Remember how long it took you to get to know their names? When you started your first job, how long did it take you to know all the departments and who did what? Well, it happened, and you were eventually able to name everyone without a second glance. Similarly, you will get to know your stones.

A thought from Mary Nelson:

In this section you will explore the sets of stones we use in Original Body of LaStone. Keep in mind that these are the beginner's sets of the heated stones and the chilled stones. I encourage you to develop your own way of working with the stones. How many stones will you need and what types of stone will you use? I personally use fifty-four heated stones, fifty-four chilled stones and twenty-seven crystals in addition to the sardonyx, the Chinese fluorite, a petoskey stone, labradorite and selenite stones. You will begin to get an idea of what stones can be incorporated into body-work; it is my hope that you forever continue to grow with the mineral kingdom and welcome their energies into your therapy sessions.

The Basalt or Heated Stones

We use different types of stone to deliver the heat during a LaStone treatment. The most common are basalt, but we also use jade. Basalt stones are dense volcanic stones. They hold their heat for a long time and release it slowly. They have energy and healing properties. We do not shape the basalt stones used; they are natural pebbles – a gift from Mother Earth. The jade does have to be shaped in order to be used.

We have stones for the neck, the toes, the face, the tummy, the spine, the chakras and much more. Nothing is left to chance – even the number fifty-four, the number of basalt stones used – is auspicious as five plus four adds up to nine. Nine is a very important number in therapy, so that is why we use it.

THE FULL SET OF HEATED STONES

1 sacral stone	12 spinal layout stones
1 belly stone	4 worker stones
1 pillow stone	8 toe stones
2 hand stones	2 face stones
10 large stones	1 third eye stone
12 medium stones	

Once you have established what constitutes an Original Body set of stones, we can go on to get to know how to recognise them and what they do. Remember that every set of Original Body stones has the same component parts. These stones are, however, naturally harvested – we only tumble them to clean them, not to change their shape. Therefore even though every set has the same type of stone, every set is totally unique in shape, colour and energy.

Your own set will be individual to you and to your clients' needs. You will eventually develop your own uses and names for your stones, and your own ways of recognising them.

HEATED STONE SET DESCRIPTIONS

Number	Size	Function	Name	Your Notes
1	Extra-large, thickest of all the stones.	Stone placement on sacral area in supine position and sacrum area in prone position.	Grandfather stone.	
1	Extra-large, thinner than grandfather stone.	Stone placement on solar plexus area in the prone position.	Grandmother stone.	
1	Extra-large, oblong stone.	Supports the occipital ridge and neck in the supine position.	Pillow stone.	
2	Extra-large, bumpy stones; usually quite chunky.	Support the hands in both supine and prone positions.	Hand stones.	
4	Oblong or pointy stones.	Used in trigger point and deep-tissue work.	Pointy stones or worker stones.	
1	Small, very smooth stone.	Used for the brow area of the forehead.	Third eye stone.	
10	Large stones: 2 thickest, 2 thick, 2 medium, 2 thin, 2 thinnest (labelled sacral placement in the set).	Used for stone placement in spinal layout, in chakra layouts and for massage on large muscle groups.	Large effleurage stones/chakra stones/sacral placement stones.	
12	Medium stones (palm size).	Used for effleurage.	Medium or pretty stones.	
12	Small stones: 4 narrow, 4 thin, 4 thick.	Used for spinal layout, supporting the curves of the spine. Four of these stones can be used in the sock in the prone position.	Spinal layout stones.	
2	Extra-small stones (very smooth).	Used for massaging the face.	Face stones.	
8	Extra, extra-small stones.	Used for placement in between in between the toes.	Toe stones.	

Heated Stones

Complete Set of Stones

The following stones are the 'odd' shaped stones; if you sort them first then the rest will be easier to find.

Abdomen/Belly and Sacrum Stones

'Grandfather/grandmother stones'. Note: The grandmother stone is flatter/thinner than the grandfather stone.

Left: grandfather sacrum stone; *Right:* grandmother belly stone

Left: grandfather sacrum stone; *Right:* grandmother belly stone (cool)

Occipital/Pillow Stone

These stones need to be large enough to fill in the cavity behind the neck, to support the neck in the supine position.

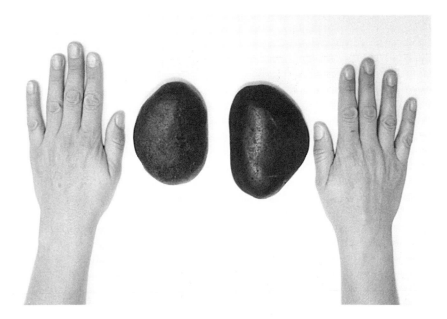

Hand Stones

Two large stones, ranging in size from a baseball to a softball size stone. They are bumpy or chunky in form.

Workers – Four Deep-tissue/Neck Stones

These stones need be long, pointy, narrow or oblong. They are for deep-tissue work and stripping in areas such as the neck. Much of the time you are using them one at a time. We try to partner/twin these stones, although this is not always possible.

One Third Eye, Two Facial and Eight Toe Stones

These are all very thin stones; the third eye is the thickest stone, followed by the toe stones. The facial stones should be smooth and flat.

Large Effleurage and Chakra Placement Stones

In the supine position:

- The four thinnest stones are used in the butterfly/spinal layout.

- The six medium-thick stones are used on the chakras.

In the prone position:

- The thickest stones can be used for stone placement on the bottoms of the feet.

- The two thinnest (sacral placement) stones are used to work the scapulas.

- All ten of the stones can be used for effleurage in the prone position.

Twelve Medium Stones for Front Effleurage

These stones are used to start the treatment with front effleurage in the supine position and for the beginning effleurage in the prone position. They can also be used in the neck area to heat up the muscles before you begin to use the deep-tissue stones for neck work if you wish to do more concentrated work. You can in fact use these stones anywhere, as they are a really universal size. They fit in the palm of your hand comfortably, which means you can manipulate them into any area you wish to work.

Twelve Small Stones for Spinal Layout

These stones are used to support the spine (along the lamina groove) in the supine position. We also add the four large stones and the pillow stone to complete 'the spinal layout'. Four of the stones can be put in a sock and placed at the back of the neck in the prone position.

Cool Stones

The marble or sardonyx used for the cool stones is less dense than the heated stones and is used to remove heat from the body. These stones are white or light in colour and are formed beneath the seabed. Their properties are phenomenal and they can be studied further in *LaStone Therapy* (*see* Further Reading, *page 184*).

There are eighteen marble or sardonyx stones in most basic sets – I say most as we source these sets from many places around the world and sometimes they vary, but normally eighteen is the number. All the stones are designed to provide cool alternatives for every hot stone we use.

The forms of the cool stones vary greatly as the stones are shaped by hand, and they vary further depending on the country from which they come. Whatever the shape, however, they all do the same job. These stones are produced for us – you very rarely find this type of stone in pebble form as it would simply break up if it tumbled on a shoreline or river bed. Each shape is carefully designed to do the most important work and to fit neatly into the therapist's hand, to enable her to switch from hot to cool in moments.

COOL STONE SET DESCRIPTIONS

Number	Size	Function	Name	Your Notes
2	Large; may be oval or round.	Used for stone placement, large muscle groups and effleurage.	Large stones.	
6	Medium; may be oval or round.	Used for stone placement, bud technique and effleurage.	Medium stones.	
6	Oblong/pointy.	Used for deep-tissue and trigger-point work.	Pointy stones.	
4	Small; may be oval or round.	Used for stone placement, effleurage and in the sock for prone position.	Small stones.	
1 Delux set	Large stone; may be oval or round.	Stone placement on sacral area in the supine position. Sacrum area or solar plexus area in the prone position.	Belly stone or grandfather or grandmother stone.	*Pictured in heated section*
1	Extra-large oblong stone.	Supports the occipital ridge and neck in the supine position.	Pillow stone.	*Pictured in heated section*

We originally only used marble for our chilled stones. Sardonyx is relatively new to us – although not to the planet, of course! This is why we have started to use it in our cool stone sets. It has amazing healing properties (*see page 37*). Your cool stone set can comprise either marble or sardonyx, or it can be a combination of both.

The easiest way to remember your chilled stones is to get to know your heated stones. This sounds odd, but it basically explains that we have a chilled/marble/sardonyx version of every basalt/jade stone we have. As you can see from the above table, there is a cool version of the sacral, belly, pillow, large, medium and small stones, and even of the toe stones and workers.

Complete Set of Cool Stones

The Other Stones in an Original Body Set

Chinese fluorite used for the Spinal Spiral technique

This stone should have a blunt point on one end and fit in your hand comfortably. It is used for the spinal spiral technique.

Legend has it that fluorite was used in carvings by both the ancient Egyptians and the Chinese. Carved fluorite artefacts have also been recovered from the Roman ruins of Pompeii, Italy. Powdered fluorite in water was used to relieve kidney disease in ancient times. It is thought by some to be beneficial for the blood vessels, spinal fluid and spleen, and to improve the absorption of vital nutrients. It may aid in fighting mental disorders, ground excess energies and promote concentration, advancing the mind to the next level of reality while balancing positive and negative aspects of the mind, resulting in spiritual awakenings.

Selenite Wands used in the Spinal Spirals

Selenite is a form of crystallised gypsum; it is for the most part clear to milky white in colour. The healing properties of this magical stone are many; it promotes success in business, provides insight into disagreements, can assist the healer in seeing disorders within the body, and supports the spinal column and movement in the muscular structure. When used in conjunction with the Chinese fluorite in the spinal spirals, the body responds in a profound way both mentally and physically. The first time I used this stone on one of my regular clients she asked, 'What are you doing?' I explained that I was doing nothing different. She then told me that she could tell that things were moving deeper within her body. It has been reported that this response happens over and over again with regular clients who have experienced the Chinese fluorite on its own and then felt the power of the stones together.

For further information, I would encourage you to read *Love is the Earth A Kaleidoscope of Crystals* by Melody, and *Stones Alive!* by Marilyn and Thomas Twintreess (*see* Further Reading, *page 184*).

Labradorite for Recharching the Stones

Labradorite is used for recharging your heated and chilled stones at the end of the day.

Legend has it that labradorite was originally discovered on the island of St Paul. Pieces of the stone were found among artefacts of the Red Painted People of Maine. Labradorite improves our ability to visualise and aids in meditations as we seek enlightenment. It offers both Yin and Yang energies to the wearer; helps in opening the heart chakra in order to more readily receive love; and enhances dreaming and the ability to remember the content of dreams during the waking hours. The stone is perfect for recharging other stones, as the results of its energies continue to build and each result enhances the next. Labradorite is the perfect stone to use when creating your altar or mosaic at the end of the day to recharge your stones (see Chapter 7).

Petoskey Stone used for the Third Eye Chakra

This is used as an alternative for the third eye stone to your heated or chilled stones.

The petoskey stone is said to dissipate negative energies, protect the head area, and stimulate the third eye and crown chakras. It blocks mischievous spirits who might try and interfere with your life. It helps you towards psychic awareness and enhances the awareness of the emotions. Petoskey stones can assist in the manifestation of your creative endeavours. I use this stone warm and placed on the third eye in the supine position. The Petoskey stone is particularly attractive; the unique designs that the coral created are a wonder to gaze at. My third eye petoskey stone is smooth and polished on one side; the other side, which lies near the skin, is natural and rough in appearance. For me this offers a balance between Yin and Yang, encouraging the third eye to open to the understanding of human form.

The Science of the Stones

When I first started to use black stones in my massage, I was curious as to what kind of stone I was using. In order to know for sure, I asked a friend who works in the US Geological Survey for the University of Arizona to help me. Bill

Updegrove was very helpful, and he and his colleagues agreed to research the stone and give me a breakdown of what they found. Chemical, mineralogical and geological questions were asked. They used a variety of methods of analysis: mass spectrometry, X-ray fluorescence, X-ray diffraction, thin-section analysis and lengthy debates that did not always end in agreement.

Listening to the results of all the research they shared with me brought me to the conclusion that this stone is one of the most common on the planet, and one of the simplest. This dismayed these professionals, who seemed to want a more spectacular stone. It was not until I explained that the simplicity of the stone made its magic even more powerful that they gave me their results.

The geologists and mineralogists found that the stones were made up of orthoclase, pyroxene, plagioclase feldspar and vitrified silicates; augite, iron and magnesium constituents were also found. The type of basalt that is used in LaStone therapy is modified igneous rock that is formed by volcanic and sedimentary action. Basalt is the most abundant of the volcanic rocks, especially plentiful in those regions that have undergone volcanic disturbance within geologically recent times. Most present-day volcanoes erupt basaltic material. This type of basalt is usually made up of polycrystalline olivine, an iron-magnesium silicate.

There are several varieties of basalt. Most contain olivine and iron-magnesium silicate, and those containing notable quantities of this mineral are known as olivine basalt. Olivine basalt is a fine-grained stone that is very dense and forms fine crystalline masses. The stones begin to form when gabbroic magma erupts as lava flows or intrudes at shallow depths to form dykes and sills. Vesicular structure is prominent at the top of the lava flow. Then gasses trapped in the cooling lava form vesicles; after solidification, secondary minerals like quartz and zeolites fill these cavities. The density of the stones is 2.5 times the weight per volume of water. The hardness is 7 on the Mohs scale of 1–10, a diamond being a 10.

The basalt that I use has been formed downwind of the volcano. These stones cooled slowly and changed composition as metamorphosis took place, and crystallised again and again, which gave them great density. Then they broke and were eroded by steam or water activity, after which they were washed along a river bottom, which gave them their smooth, potato-like shape and size. From the information I have gained I have concluded that this is why the stones high in iron and magnesium stay hotter longer than any of the other stones Mother Earth has to offer. Basalt is found all over Mother Earth, wherever there has been volcanic action – you need only to go out and search your area to find it.

The healing properties of basalt stones are stability and strength, clarity in difficult times; the stones can ease anger and promote understanding in such situations. Basalt has also been said to enhance the reproductive system and increase fertility.

Stones used in the Chilled Application

Organic rocks such as marble and sardonyx come from living organisms. They are formed directly or indirectly from materials that were once living and are made up of mostly calcite and limestone. Calcite is colourless or white when pure, but may be of almost any colour, including varying shades of red, pink, yellow, green, blue, lavender, black or brown, owing to the presence of diverse impurities, or sugar veins. It may be transparent, translucent or opaque. Its lustre ranges from vitreous to dull. Calcite is number 3 on the Mohs hardness scale; it can be scratched readily by a knife.

Most fresh water and seawater contains dissolved calcium carbonate. All limestone is formed when the calcium carbonate crystallises out of solution, or from the skeletons of small sea urchins and coral. Limestone is a rock made of calcite. Most limestone is grey, but all colours of limestone, from white to black, have been found. Deposits of limestone are typically formed from the shells of creatures such as clams and certain micro-organisms. The shells collect on the ocean floor, accumulate and compress into rock over time. Some sedimentary rocks are formed when a sea or lake dries up, leaving large amounts of dissolved minerals that then concentrate and form a solid. Marble is formed by the alteration of limestone by heat and pressure. The calcite in the limestone changes and fossils and layering in the original limestone disappear as interlocking grains grow. If the limestone is pure, a white marble is formed. Limestones may include layers of clay or sand, which may form the attractive sugar veins (colours) found in marble.

All stones are vulnerable to scratching. A highly polished surface on an organic stone (marble, limestone, sardonyx) is more likely to show signs scratching than a mineral stone (basalt) will. The organic stones, which are principally calcium based, rank 3 on the Mohs hardness scale, while basalt ranks 6–7. But over time, both will acquire signs of use that are essentially an accumulation of tiny scratches. These scratches do not bother most of us who are familiar with the properties of the stones – we accept them as the natural consequence of time and use.

Marble is used for protection; many altars are made of marble for this purpose. It is also said to aid in personal success and body fitness. It is common knowledge that marble is the stone of choice to adorn castles, churches or any building that is a place of honour and authority. Marble will assist in recalling your dreams and promotes meditation. In relationships it supports common sense and matters of the heart.

EXERCISE

Write a small description of the stones we heat, stating what are they made of, and make a list of the shapes there are in a set, and what are they used for. Write a short description of the stones we cool, and list the types and the shapes we use. Name the other types of stone used in the treatment, and describe what are they used for.

CHAPTER 6

Arranging the Heated and Chilled Stones

KEY POINTS

- We place stones in a certain way to save time for our clients – we don't waste valuable treatment time 'looking' for our stones.

- Over the years we have revised the way we place the stones in the heating unit. This will probably keep on developing and changing long into the future, but for now, our recommended way to place your stones is as described here.

- Bear in mind that a common complaint involving novice LaStone therapists is along the lines of 'my therapist seemed to spend a lot of time looking in the tank, while I was on the table waiting for the wonderful stones'.

- As soon as we finish with a stone and go to place it back 'on temperature', we must move efficiently and swiftly. Having a system for your stones aids this process.

The Heated Stones

We need to do everything we can to reduce the time 'off' the body. We use stone bags and a 'roaster layout' for this purpose.

The Stone Bags

To hold the stones, we use three main bags, and one sock or net; we also have some stones loose in the heater. Here is how this works:

- Bag 1 contains *all the stones that go **under** your client.*

- Bag 2 contains *all the stones that go **on** your client.*

- Bag 3 contains *all the stones for the face, neck and decollette.*

- The sock or net contains *all your toe stones.*

We also have stones in the tank ready and waiting for when the bags have been emptied and placed.

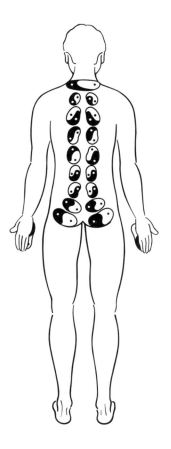

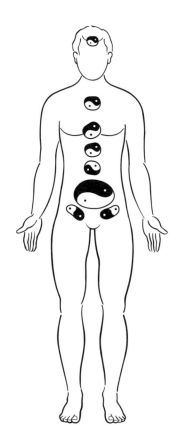

Spinal Layout – Bag 1
All the stones that go *under*
your client.

Chakra Placement – Bag 2
All the stones that go *on*
your client

Bag 1

In the diagrams above and in further detail in the section explaining the treatment, you will see that we lay our client on a 'spinal layout' (of stones) at the very start of the session. In order to do this efficiently and quickly, we put all the stones we need for this into one bag, which is Bag 1.

Bag 2

We also put stones on our client in the chakra placement (*see page 40*). So that we can do this without leaving the client (we are using energy connection at this stage), we place all the stones we want to use together in one bag, Bag 2.

Bag 3

We normally work on the face without moving away during the sequence. If we do a facial we have all the tools we need on a table or trolley next to the client. We massage the client by making contact and carrying out the whole sequence. When working around the head and face it is best not to move around too much as this can be disruptive to the client. We therefore put all the stones we are going to use in the face, neck, shoulders and front of chest sequence in one bag. We take this bag to the head of our client and do the whole session with all the stones we need to hand. These are the stones in Bag 3.

Sock or net

The little toe stones are fab; they are also small, and can hide under the other stones – they think it's fun to do this! Well, we don't think it's much fun to use valuable time trying to fish out eight mischievous little stones when we are trying to do a great treatment so we keep 'em all together in one baby sock or fishing net. Problem solved – they cannot hide . . .

The Loose Stones

We have some stones that are mature and sensible and are fine to let loose in the tank. They include the belly stone and the medium stones, the twelve stones we use to do the bulk of the effleurage work. These take on the responsibility of working on and relaxing our client throughout the treatment; they are happy to sit and wait until they are needed – free in the tank.

SUMMARY

Bag 1	Bag 2	Bag 3	Sock/net
12 spinal layout stones	6 large stones	4 worker stones	8 toe stones
2 large 'thinnest' stones	Sacral stone	2 face stones	
(sacral placement)	Third eye stone		
2 large thin stones			
1 pillow stone			

OPTIONAL

2 hand stones

(These can be left loose in the heater.)

Remaining stones in heater

12 medium effleurage stones

Belly stone

Hand stones if not placed in Bag 1

Water Heater Layout

Now that we have our stones in their bags, we need to have a system to know where they are in the water heater. Depending on the shape of your heater you could be working with an oblong, a square or a circle.

Whatever the shape of your heater, the best way to lay out the stones in the heater is to:

- Place the belly stone in the middle of the tank as you don't need it until later (when you turn your client over).

- Position bags 1, 2 and 3 from right to left. It is then easy to pick them out of the tank from left to right.

- The sock or net goes in wherever you want to put it.

- The twelve medium stones go all along the sides (their exact placement will depend on the shape of your tank).

- As soon as the stones are in the tank, you can pour in the water to cover them and turn the power on. Be sure to check the individual operating instructions for your tank. Always put the water in after you have positioned the stones in the tank – if you do it the other way round you will not know how much water to use.

Your stones are now ready to be heated.

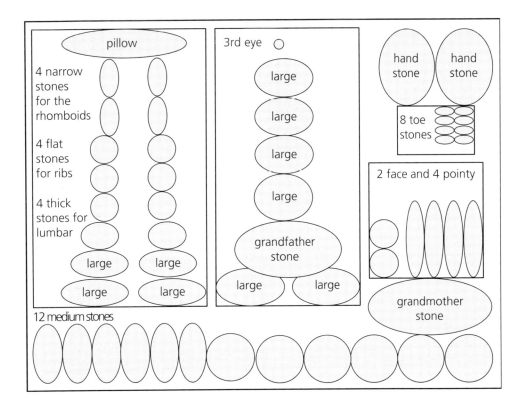

A message from Mary Nelson:

It is very important that you place your heated stones in the heating unit in the same position after each time you use them, and return them to the heating unit after every use. If you do not follow a system for yourself you will waste precious moments during the treatment. On the next few pages are the methods that I have created to make use of time, allowing me to be more efficient during a treatment.

Sometime in 1999 I was blessed with teaching an unsighted person; I will refer to her as Liz. Teena Pleshek was a teacher-in-training at the time and was assisting me at this workshop. Initially we said, 'How were we going to help Liz find her stones in the heating unit without burning herself?' Then Teena came up with a plan. She ran home and brought back with her five or six orange net bags – you know, the kind oranges are sold in at supermarkets. We sorted out the stones with Liz, grouping them in sets that would allow her to retrieve her stones from the heating unit with ease. The orange bags worked like a charm and to our surprise Liz had her stones all memorised by the end of the first day. That night when Liz's husband came to pick her up, we spoke to him about the heating unit and what could be done to protect Liz from the hot edges of the unit. He said that he would build a wooden box to fit over the unit; Liz could touch the sides of the box and then be able to feel her way into the heating unit, where her bags of stones would be waiting for her.

This workshop with Liz also offered us additional information, for as I watched Liz feel her stones and discover what size was for what technique. I realised that she was able to do this much better than anyone I had ever watched before. At this moment I knew that from that day forward I would blindfold the students on the first day of their training, so that they could explore their stones without their eyes, but with their touch, their intuition. The transformation that took place in Liz, Teena and myself is still to this day being experienced. All who enter the world of stone massage through our teachings have been blessed with the gift of internal sight. We were all very pleased with the outcome of this first day with Liz, our angel in disguise.

I shared the experience that Teena and I had with other instructors. I explained how Liz found her stones so much faster then anyone else, how the orange bags worked for her and the fun we had figuring it all out. Tomi Wertheim took the 'net bag method' into her very next workshop and had rave reviews. The other instructors and I incorporated the blindfold game right away and struggled with the idea of net bags. We just did not want to stop using the layout for the heating unit; the bags seemed ugly and they surely did not allow you to see the beauty of the stones lying in the warm water.

About a year later I gave in and began to experiment with net bags – with which stones to put in which bag. How many bags did I need to allow for more efficient results in the organisation of a sixty-or ninety-minute treatment? Are the net bags the same for the supine position as for the prone position? For myself the net bags work wonderfully on the supine side of the body. I do, however, prefer not to use the net bags when working on the client's back. I am in and out of the heating unit so much and so fast that the bags are a nuisance to me. In the prone position I place the stones in a 'medicine wheel' formation, always keeping the twins side by side so that I might use them together and in sequence.

I do teach with the net bags for both the supine and the prone position. I find that this works best for the students because they only use a few stones at a time and do not need to retrieve stones as fast as I do when I work privately.

It is my hope that you embrace the concept of the net bags while learning your stones. Each stone will perform specific jobs for you, offer a vibration to the client and balance its twin as you use them together. Every stone has unique markings; they each have a story to tell. In the book *Other Council Fires Were Here Before Ours* by Jamie Sams and Twylah Nitsch (*see* Further Reading, *page 184*), there is a chapter called 'The Language of the Stones'. There you can study the markings that are on stones and their meanings as offered to the human race. Your set of heated stones has a 'reading' for you; take time to learn what that message is.

I offer you the net bag concept; this will provide you with added minutes in your treatments. I am very pleased that Liz came to us and offered us this form of learning. She opened our eyes to seeing more internally, allowing the stones to become a part of us through touch.

To Cool Your Stones

There are many ways to cool your stones and you will probably change the method depending on the facilities you have to hand.

You can use:

Ice	Ice-cold water
A freezer	Ice blocks
A fridge	A sandwich cooler
A bowl of 'slush ice'	A cool box

- Use any way you can to get your stones as cool as you need for your client. There will be pros and cons to whatever method you use.

- Ice is good and efficient, and even more so with a little water added (think champagne bucket – there is always water in the ice to totally cover the bottle to chill quickly).

- You can freeze your stones but you need access to frozen stones for each treatment as they take longer to cool and the freezer needs to be near by.

- A fridge is the same as a freezer but a little slower still.

- Slush ice in a bowl is great as it is quiet, sits around the stones and looks great – but it melts quickly so you need a constant supply.

- Ice-cold water is similar to slush ice; it needs refreshing constantly and you have to be careful not to get everything wet.

- Ice blocks are good and placing them in an insulated cooler will keep them very cold. They will, however, take longer to cool the stones.

- A sandwich cooler or cool box is good; make sure you keep the lid on it. You will probably need to use a secondary source of cold to keep the stones very cool before use.

- If you have a chiller cabinet in your treatment room, and a good supply of stones, this is great. Beware, however, of the noise of the door mechanism or handle disturbing the peace.

You basically need to select a method from the above list of keeping your stones cool. They don't need to be positioned in any pattern, but you do need to be able to see them. If, for instance, you have white stones on clear ice in a white cooler, it will be difficult for you to see them and you may generate too much noise scrabbling around to find the stone you want. Make sure you put the marble stones against a coloured background so that you can see them clearly.

More thoughts from Mary Nelson:

When possible I chill my marble, sardonyx, jade and quartz stones in a freezer; if one is not available then I use ice. The reason I do not use ice for the most part is due to the noise that ice makes when you are retrieving the stones from a freezer unit. Everyone knows what it sounds like to reach into an ice chest for a cold drink; we all know that if a can is under the ice it hurts a bit to find your drink. The memory of this can be aroused within the client when they hear you fetching your chilled stones from the ice, which in turn may cause them alarm or concerns of the 'how cold is that stone going to be anyway?' kind.

On the other hand if you only have eighteen to twenty stones, you will need to use ice. It takes too long for the marble, sardonyx and quartz to rechill in the freezer once you have used them on your client. In a bowl of ice and a little water they will come back to 32 degrees Fahrenheit (0 degrees Celsius) within minutes and you can use the same stone over and over again.

In addition to my fifty-four heated stones, I use a mixture of fifty-four marble, sardonyx and quartz stones within a ninety-minute LaStone treatment. I suggest that over time you consider purchasing additional marble, sardonyx and quartz stones, especially if you are using chilled stones in the spinal and chakra layouts, and for chilled application to the body. They make great holiday gifts, so put a bug in your family's ear about what you might want for the next special occasion.

Once your stones are at the correct temperature you are ready to go.

EXERCISE

Draw the outline of three large bags and one small one. Draw inside the stones that belong in each bag. There are some stones that do not have a bag but have their own spot in the tank. What are they and where do they go?

Care and Maintenance of Stones and Equipment

KEY POINTS

- You must wash and season your heated stones before use.

- You must wash and dry your chilled stones before use.

- You must use a technique to sterilise your stones during and between treatments.

- You must clean your stones at the end of every day, even if they have only been used once.

- You must recharge your stones every day in some way.

- You must store your stones at the end of each day.

- You must treat your stones with respect; they are the tools of your trade.

- You must wash and rinse both your heating system and your cooling system at the end of every day of use.

- You should keep your towels, sheets and other laundry clean and hygienic for your clients.

- Always wipe excess oil from your massage table, equipment and work-station. If the oil is allowed to build up it is much harder to clean up and looks and is unprofessional.

● You should always be happy for anyone to see your stones, equipment and work area. If you clean as you go you will save time and keep safe with no surprises.

Care of Your Stones

We use many different stones and crystals during a LaStone treatment. You must take care of your stones and crystals, as they are the tools of your trade. Keeping them clean, hygienic and in good condition is imperative to a successful and healing treatment. Keeping your stones recharged and full of energy isn't an option; it is a must. Whatever stone you are using – basalt, marble, jade, sardonyx, quartz, calcedy, petoskey, fluorite, labradorite, selenite – you must look after them and they in turn will look after you.

The Heated Stones

When the basalt stones are new they are lighter in colour than the dark, polished look you may be familiar with from photographs. Don't worry– very soon your stones will look just the same: gloriously deep in colour with a smooth sheen. When new, the stones are also dry and hold no moisture. They have a slightly porous surface and need to be seasoned and sealed, just as a new cast-iron pan or wok would be.

Before your stones do massages for you, you must prepare them by giving them a treatment. Think of this as a way of getting to know them in preparation for a long and successful partnership.

To begin with, bathe the stones in warm, soapy water and let them dry. Then oil the stones one by one; take time to get to know them – learn the curves, crevasses and markings that have formed over the eons. You can blend a special massage oil or you can simply use a plain carrier oil. Use this time to see the colours and shapes and begin to recognise your own stones.

Your instructor will take you through this preparation if you are at a class – oiling the stones, leaving them out to dry and using them in treatments. If you receive your stones before or after a course, you will need to do the following:

Wash your new stones in hot, soapy water and leave them to dry. Just as you like to take a shower after a long journey or flight, so do the dusty stones.

Oil the stones in your own chosen blend of natural oils. After our refreshing bath or shower we should always moisturise to keep our skin looking and feeling good.

Check your stones regularly. Most stones are used with oil in a body-massage treatment, but a few are not. These stones are kept for placement or work over fabric – they include the sacral stone, the belly stone and the hand stones. They may dry more quickly as they are placed in water every day but not oiled. Keep an eye on them, and if they need a little tender loving care and a good moisturising – then treat them.

Your stones could get little chips knocked off them if you drop them or carry them together. It is worth checking for this by smoothing around your stones with your hands once in a while – especially if you have dropped them on a solid floor – to make sure you do not scratch your clients. Note that it is extremely difficult to damage basalt as any weakness would probably already have been found in the thousands of years worth of natural tumbling, but it does happen – if your sacral stone lands on a toe stone, just cross your fingers and hope both stones were strong enough to take the knock!

Your Chilled Stones

Your chilled stones are a slightly different matter from your heated stones. They are very porous and much softer and as such, need to have all the oil removed from them at the end of every day and to be treated like the best cut-glass. If any oil is left on the marble stones it will be absorbed by them, and the stones will become softer and will chip and break more easily.

Also, you may find that the marble stones begin to discolour. They will start out bright and white, and as the oils used in massage are generally yellow or green in colour so the marble will become yellowed. This is not a problem – it is to be expected and is not a fault. If you use highly coloured aromatherapy oils – orange or blue ones, for example – your chilled stones may even take on a rainbow effect!

When you open your box of marble stones, see how they are wrapped and keep up that level of protection. They will just need a cool rinse and will be ready to go. At the end of every day of use, wash the stones in hot soapy water and leave them to recharge (see below). If any oil remains on the stones, use the surgical spirit or alcohol solution to break it down.

Recharging and Energising Your Stones

Just as we like to go home to shower and change at the end of a long day of treatments, so too do the stones. If someone was to close the therapy room door and leave you in the dark all night, hot and oily, until the morning, it would not be a pretty sight that greeted your first client of the day.

So, wash your stones and clean your equipment every day and it will always be fresh and raring to go. If you don't care for your stones they will soon will feel tired and neglected, and have no energy left to do a good job. They need to recharge their batteries in exactly the same way that we need to recharge ourselves by, for example, going out with friends.

There are many ways to recharge or energise your stones. If you do not do this your stones will misbehave. Take care of them and they will take care of you. If your stones are not staying hot or will not heat up despite your heater showing a reading of over 55 degrees, they are telling you they need a bit of TLC! Here's how you can go about recharging your stones.

Using labradorite for heated or moonstone for chilled stones

We use labradorite (also called spectralite) crystals to recharge the heated stones, and can also use moonstone to recharge the chilled stones – although labradorite will do the job for both quite adequately. Placing a piece of any of these crystals with your stones ensures that the stones remain neutral and cleansed during and in between treatments.

The characteristics of labradorite

Labradorite is a beautiful dark crystal with blue or green flashes of iridescent colour. Spiritually, this crystal helps us to see our goals and intentions. It helps with intuition, and tuning into our own intuition. Emotionally labradorite brings up forgotten memories and gives us depth of feeling. It stimulates our imagination and makes us contemplative and introspective. Mentally labradorite helps us to develop a child-like enthusiasm, and many new ideas. It makes us more creative. Physically labradorite alleviates colds and flu, rheumatic illness and gout. It is calming, and can help to lower blood pressure.

Essentially, labradorite is a crystal for wisdom. It is a protective stone, deflecting unwanted energies from the aura and preventing energy leakage. It aligns physical and etheric bodies, raises consciousness and grounds spiritual energy into the body; it synthesises intellectual thought with intuitive wisdom, and accesses spiritual purpose; it regulates the metabolism; it gives us insight without searching, and it protects our aura during meditation or energy work – as does fluorite.

The characteristics of moonstone

We use moonstone to charge the marble stones as it is a female stone to the masculine labradorite. As its name suggests, it is aligned to the moon and is therefore associated with intuition, fertility and the heart. Spiritually it encourages medium abilities and dreams. Emotionally moonstone refines our perception and intuition. It allows us to remember our dreams, helps to diffuse anger and balances emotional overreaction. Mentally it opens us to sudden or irrational impulses. It encourages serendipity. Physically moonstone balances hormonal production and nature's rhythms within the body. It can enhance fertility and help with menstrual problems both during and after childbirth. It can also calm the digestion and be fabulously detoxifying.

Using natural salt for recharging

Salt is a natural substance and element created by the earth or the sea. It helps to neutralise and cleanse the stones. You can sprinkle salt on your heated stones or place the stones on top of natural salt for recharging.

It is nice to scatter natural sea salt on your stones, because it is cleansing and balancing, and we also know that salt was an extremely rare and valuable substance in years gone by. You should never place your marble stones on salt as it will be absorbed by the stones and soften them. This will make your marble stones more likely to split or crack.

Using sage for recharching

You can alternatively use natural or wild sage with the stones. Sage is an extremely cleansing plant used in many Native American rituals.

Using the energy of the moon and sun for recharging

Just as we like to go home occasionally to see friends or at the end of each day to our families, so do the stones. They came from the earth and were exposed to the elements as they were forming and changing ready for us to use them. So, getting the stones back to the earth is a great way to recharge them.

The earth resonantes to a natural rhythm and so do the stones – getting the stones back to nature or outside into the elements helps them 'tune in' to their normal resonance and frequency. Leaving your stones outside once a month for twenty-four hours will recharge them with both sun and moon energy (Yin and Yang: perfect balance again).

Using mandalas or medicine wheels for recharging

Placing the stones somewhere in a pattern or picture with the intention of recharging them will keep your stones happy on a daily basis. You can recharge your stones by putting them in a mandala or medicine wheel on the massage couch or plinth, or in a space in the treatment area. Using the mandala is a way of honouring flow and energy, and leaving the stones in some form of pattern or design will help them to recharge.

Many cultures use mandalas, or circles, to represent the total circle of life, birth and then ceaseless spinning to death, which gives rise to birth, and is followed by death, and so on. Phrases such as 'circle of life' and 'this mortal coil' show how we think of life as either a visual or actual circle or sphere.

Native Americans use mandalas to represent the wheel of life. The Native American mandala is also called a medicine wheel. This wheel is marked out into the compass points, north, south, east and west; the four seasons, spring, summer, autumn and winter; and the four elements, water, earth, air and fire.

It seems that whatever your belief, you can use the imagery of the circle and the power of nature to create your own personal mandala or medicine wheel. It enables you to focus on your own life, beliefs and path to achieve and create whatever you wish. It is the same for the stones, reflection and regeneration.

Cleaning Your Stones

You need to make sure you wash the stones every time you have finished with them, and give them fresh water every day you use them. Don't stew them in old, dirty water overnight, and don't put them in the dishwasher. If they are sticky, then surgical spirit or alcohol solution is the quickest way to get the oil off.

Obviously you cannot take all the stones out of the heater and cooler in between each treatment. This would take far too long and would be unnecessary. Keep the heated stones hygienic and safe during the day by placing a sterilising tablet or solution in the water tank at the start of the day. This will ensure that anything that survives the heat of the water will be destroyed or neutralised by the solution. The marble stones are generally on ice or in a cooler, so you cannot employ the same technique for them. The easiest way to keep your marble stones clean is to spray them with surgical spirit or a sterilising solution in between each session. As you use your marble stones, or at the end of each treatment, simply spray the stones with the cleansing solution before placing them back in the cooler for the next treatment.

Take care and enjoy your stones!

From Mary Nelson (on what happens if you don't recharge your stones):

I invite you to challenge this belief of mine and see if your stones don't lose their lustrous appearance and ability to hold in heat and cold. You and your stones will become tired and lack excitement about your work together. You will have to exchange the heated stones more often due to the fact that there won't be enough heat in one stone to do the work you are trying to accomplish. The cold stones will begin to feel sticky and lifeless. The spirit of the stones will have slipped away somewhere and your clients will no longer comment on how incredible the treatment is with the stones.

At this point I pray that you remember my words and take all your stones (every stone or crystal you own) outside and give thanks for their time and the energies that they are so willing to share with you. Only then will the life of the stones come back to you in your work. The excitement of collecting your stones from outside the next morning will be similar to that experienced by, say, getting a new puppy or opening up a special present. You will have been energised, as well as the stones, and you will work happily together once more. Only if you can believe in this connection with the stones and Mother Earth will you prosper in your business. So open your heart to the healing powers within the stones and you and your clients will soar further than your dreams have taken you so far.

Care of Your Equipment

The stones need cleansing and recharging, and your equipment needs cleaning at the end of each day too. If you let oil residue build up on any object, it will become unhygienic, sticky and smelly. If, on the other hand, you take care of your equipment, it will last longer and you will therefore be saving money.

Some further information on maintaining your stones from Mary Nelson:

The use of crystals, salts, the sun, the moon and water helps to bring back the energy lost by the stones when they are doing their work on clients. Useful references for stones' energies are *Other Council Fires Were Here Before Ours* by Jamie Sams and Twylah Nitsch; *Crystal, Gem & Metal Magic* by Scott Cunningham; *Love Is In The Earth: Laying-On-Of-Stones* by Melody;   by Katrina Raphael, and *Stones Alive!* by Marilyn and Thomas Twintreess.

I cannot emphasise this enough: you must clean and store your stones daily. If you don't give thanks for what the stones have done for you during the day, they will lose their energies. This is a fact – you can look at it as electromagnetic energy or you can open your heart and see it as I do. The Stone People do an enormous amount of healing work for us during our work. They not only balance, ground and aid in healing our clients; they also heal our hands, thumbs and wrists.

If you do not take the time to practise certain ceremonies for the stones on a daily basis, they will lose their inner energies. They will not stay hot/cold for you during your work. You will wonder if your roaster isn't keeping the stones hot any longer, and begin to raise the thermostat, thinking something is wrong, not realising that all you need to do is to get the stones outside in their element. The stones love to be outside in water or lying on the earth and bathing in the moonlight.

A note of caution – if you are lucky enough to put your stones outside during an electrical storm, beware, for the stones soak up a great deal of energy during a storm and will be much hotter than usual for the next treatments. My clients always comment on how hot the stones are after a storm; even though I don't change the setting on the roaster, the stones are energised . . . they love to be outside during a storm or a full moon.

All the stones used in LaStone are energised in the same way. Clients don't seem to mind the increase in the cold after the chilled stones have been energised, for if you use the cold stones on areas of inflammation, as they should be used, then the extra cold is welcomed and soaked into the body for healing purposes.

This language of the stones contains stories and messages to us, the two-legged creatures walking on Mother Earth. I suggest you read Jamie Sams and Twylah Nitsch's book *Other Council Fires Were Here Before Ours* on this subject. Apart from containing enlightening information on why the stones are willing to aid people on their life paths, the back of the book has a section that includes drawings and descriptions of the markings on the bodies of the Stone People. These natural markings bring power to the carrier or user of the stones. So read about the language of the Stone People and you will learn to listen even more to the powerful messages the stones have for you.

The following is a letter that AML Stone Source received from a student in regard to the set of stones she purchased from them.

Dear Sheila and T.J.,

Hopefully this letter finds you in the best of health and high spirits! I am writing a brief letter to share my thoughts a bit, and to thank you for my recent set of stones. The shapes are familiar as I unwrap them, and their characters and spirits appeal to me like we have forever known one another. As I lay all of the stone-filled plastic bags around my kitchen sink filling with water, preparing the bathing ritual, the toe stones jump into the water, and this does not surprise me – that these babies are especially anxious and active, and not content just to wait for me to get to them.

As the back effleurage stones lie in the bottom of my sink with the water draining out, they exude a sense of joyousness as the water falls from their sides. I have the idea that they would love a shower; so I turn on the water to the kitchen sink hose, and use the spray nozzle to drizzle them for a few moments; they could have stayed under that showering for hours (these babies have hedonistic tendencies). As I arrange the entire set to dry on a tea towel on my kitchen work-surface, they visibly expand with breaths; the sighs that come with relaxing into a fuzzy robe and slippers after a bubble bath. I sprinkle them with kosher salt. Their first night must be indoors. I burn camphor and place lit candles among them. The lights in the room are turned off. Too bad my camera was not available; it is quite a beautiful sight. Such a spiritual connection; we are thrilled to have each other! Tomorrow I will anoint them with oil; I will massage them before they massage anyone else. These stones have a great home, and this is an ideal partnership.

Thank you!

Amy Storm, Washington D.C.

EXERCISE

Write out a 'clean-up' plan and a recharging schedule. Find a diary with moon cycle details.

Note that if you get into a routine at the end of each day, you will soon find that tidying up can be done efficiently in just a short period of time. Leaving your stones to recharge in a regular way makes sure that they are energised and ready to go – and you are tidied up and ready too. The more energy your stones have, the less work you will be required to do and the more effective the treatment will be for your client.

CHAPTER 8

Temperature Control and Troubleshooting

KEY POINTS

- The LaStone treatment can use many different temperatures; you must find a way to be accurate in heating and cooling the stones.

- You should find out how long all your equipment and stones take to get to the right temperature in order to avoid delay before or during treatments.

- Check all electrical equipment regularly for wear and tear.

- Learn how long your equipment takes to heat a used stone.

- Learn how long your equipment takes to cool a used stone.

- If something isn't right, fix it.

There are many different methods of heating and cooling the stones. Some systems have thermostats, some have naked flames; all can be controlled so that the temperature is accurate. Check the instructions with your equipment and get to know how it works.

Thermometer

Having a thermometer to hand is important. It allows you to confirm the temperature of your water at any time.

Calibrating the thermometer

If your heating system requires a thermometer it is essential that you use one that is accurate in order to monitor the temperature of the water even if the heating unit itself has a gauge for adjusting the degrees (for instance to low, medium and high). The calibration of a given heating unit can vary, so you can only trust a thermometer to know the exact temperature of the water heating your stones.

It will be necessary for you to calibrate your thermometer every day as well. To do this make sure your thermometer has the ability to be calibrated. There is usually a small nut at the base of the thermometer that will allow you to adjust it by turning it with a wrench. To calibrate a thermometer you will need ice with a little water, with the water being at 32°F/0°C. Place the thermometer in the ice and water and, using the nut with a wrench, move the dial of the thermometer to read 32°F/0°C. This will ensure that when you place the thermometer in the hot water it will give you an accurate reading of how hot the water truly is. There is no other way to be sure of the accuracy of the water temperature. You can also check the temperature of the chilling unit/freezer for your marble stones in this way. Keep in mind that the iced water should be at 32°F/0°C when cooling your marble and sardonyx stones.

Heating Your Stones

Place the stones in a heating unit that holds enough water to cover the tops of all the stones. Place the stones on a white background or hand towel; the towel will protect the bottom of the heating unit and soften the noise the stones make as you put them in and take them out of the unit. The white background will also enable you to see the stones in a darkened room.

Most heating units have an insert or shelves; place the stones in the insert and fill with water. Then adjust the temperature control of the heater as needed. If it is a new heater or one you are unfamiliar with, make sure you know how long it takes to get to the required temperature for your stones. You don't want to be in a situation where you and your client are ready, but the stones are cold.

When you place several stones that are at a neutral temperature back in the heating unit it will be necessary to increase the heat for a few minutes or wait to use them again to give the tank time to bring them back to the correct temperature. You can do this in two ways. One way is to allow time for the stones to reach the correct temperature naturally in the water without touching the dial and adjusting the temperature control. It will take about three to four minutes for the stones to reheat this way. Or you can place the lid back on the heating unit and turn the temperature dial up just a little bit. However, if you choose the latter method you will need to remember to remove the lid and adjust the dial control before going on with the session in order to avoid ending up with stones that are too hot. Keep in mind that germs start to die at high temperatures; if you use an oxidiser in the water as well as maintaining the water temperature above 110°F/43°C you will be operating in a safe zone as far as sanitation procedures go with water to the body.

If the stones are too hot and the heating unit is set at the temperature that usually maintains the correct temperature for you, make sure there is enough water in the roaster. The less water, the hotter the stones may get. During different times of the year the control for the temperature will vary due to the temperature in the room. A water temperature range of 110°F/43°C to 140°F/60°C allows you to hold the stones comfortably in your hands and be at the range of temperatures for any considerations you will need to be mindful of for clients with contraindications. If the stones are not warm and the water heater is set at the correct temperature and you have checked it with your thermometer, then you should look at recharging your stones; they may just be exhausted.

Again, the only way you will know the temperature of the water and the stones for sure is by using a thermometer that you have calibrated at the beginning of the day.

Marble, sardonyx and quartz stones – from Mary Nelson:

Place them in a bucket of ice or a small freezer; I have a dorm-size freezer unit in my office. On ice it only takes fifteen minutes to get the stones cold enough to use; in the freezer it may take as much as one hour. It is important to know the temperature of your stones, just as it is to know how hot the basalt stones are. You can use the same type of thermometer for the freezer; just remember to calibrate it as you do for the hot water. If you place your stones over ice make sure there is enough ice to form a bed of ice in the container, and not just some ice in a lot of water.

I use chilled stones on areas of recent injuries, burns and inflammation. The chilled stones remove the heat from the body, allowing the client to relax the injured area. I use the cold/cool stones for trigger-point and cross-fibre friction, as well as just laying them on or tucking them in where they are needed. The chilled stones penetrate far deeper than any other form of ice treatment I have ever used. Be careful not to stay in one area too long; it is possible to burn some-one with cold as well as with heat. Clients' responses to the heated and chilled stones are far more positive than when you use hydrocolators, heating pads or ice as in cryotherapy work.

Once you finish an application of chilled stones to the body and need to return to using warm stones, be mindful that your hands are cold and will not feel the depth of heat coming from a hot stone. Take care, therefore, when applying a fresh hot stone on the client if your hands are cold. I dip my hands in hot water for a few seconds to warm up them up before using heated stones after I have used cold stones.

Before you replace the stones on the ice or in the freezer, it will be necessary for you to clean them off with some kind of anti-bacterial agent. I presently use alcohol, for it is quick to dry and has been recognised by the medical field as a cleaning agent. I do understand that many individuals do not agree with this finding; if you feel this way, use any method you can create to quickly rinse the marbles stones off before you return them to the ice or freezer. This is absolutely necessary when using the cold stones.

If you are placing your stones in a freezer it is necessary for you to dry them off before you place them back in the unit; if you don't do this the stones will stick to one another and it is hard to separate them when they are frozen together.

The following chart is aimed at helping you with some troubleshooting con-cerns you might come across during your practice with LaStone therapy. Working with the stones is a magical experience for both you and your client; it is my wish for you that you find a rhythm with the stones, and the temperatures, and bring balance to your work with the vibrations the stones have to offer you and your client. Try not to be in your head too much with this work, but allow your heart and intuition to guide you with the dance of the stones. It is certainly important to understand the science of the stones, but surely the reason why the stones awoke on the planet at this time was to bring balance and a connection with Mother Earth and her human children. So go forth and experiment with the science, but also find a way to play as a child would in the waters of the sea.

The Problem	The Solutions
Stones are too hot to hold.	Check your water temperature, and adjust it if need be. • Add cool water to the heating unit. • Dip the hot stones in cool water for a split second; this will change their temperature rapidly. • Squirt alcohol or a cooling agent over the stones. • Set the stones on the massage table for a moment while you access the muscle you want to apply them to. • It is possible to cool the stones off while doing effleurage, using firm, deep pressure with adequate speed to allow the heat to penetrate the client's muscles and underlining tissue. • Do not forget to dry off the stones before you bring them to the massage table.
Stones are not hot enough.	• Increase the heating unit control temperature. • Put the lid on the heating unit. • Monitor these adjustments every two or three minutes; the stones will heat up fast. • Use a different stone until the others heat up.
Stones are too cold.	• Set the stones on the massage table for a moment while you access the muscle you want to apply them to. • Do not forget to dry off the stones before you bring them to the massage table.
Stones keep falling off the client's body.	• Leave them off. • Use stones that are of the opposite temperature.
It is difficult to make the stones stay in certain locations.	• Use a tube sock for the hot stones, for behind the neck. • Use a woman's trouser sock for the cold stones, for behind the neck. • Use a pillowcase to wrap around joints. • Place the stones in the sock or pillowcase and wrap the whole unit around or over the area you want to isolate the temperature in. • Note that the hotter a stone is the thicker the material needs to be; the cooler the stone the thinner the material needs to be.

The Problem	The Solutions
The client says the stones are too hot in the spinal layout.	<ul><li>Find out if all the stones are too hot or just one or two.</li><li>If one or two stones are hot, pull them out and slip them under one more layer of sheet.</li><li>If the stone you just adjusted is still too hot, remove it and replace with a chilled stone.</li><li>If all the stones are too hot, immediately sit the client up and then add one more pillowcases.</li></ul>
The client says the stones are too hot on the front chakra(s).	<ul><li>Replace the hot stones with chilled ones; remember to do this with the client's breath and demonstrating honour and respect for the separating and joining of a stone to the body.</li></ul>
The front chakra stones are too heavy.	<ul><li>If they are basalt/hot stones replace them with marble/chilled stones.</li><li>If they are marble/chilled stones, first try replacing them with smaller chilled stones.</li><li>If a small chilled stone is still too heavy try holding the stone and the chakra together and send blessings of love and light into that chakra.</li><li>You can also take another stone and draw circles or figure-eights on the stone; this sings the song of the stones, and the vibration is most welcomed by the client's body and soul.</li><li>Remember to do this with the client's breath and demonstrating honour and respect for the separating and joining of a stone to the body.</li></ul>
The toe stones keep falling out.	<ul><li>Leave them out.</li></ul>
The third eye stone won't stay on.	<ul><li>You may want to have a few different shapes of third eye stones.</li><li>There are a few foreheads that just won't hold a third eye stone; in that case I hold my palm there gently and rest for a moment before completing the spiral opening or energy connection.</li><li>If there is room on the table, you can set the third eye stone on the massage table tucked into the client's hair at the top of their head.</li></ul>
The stones didn't go back in the hot water and you don't have the stone/size to use for the heated application you were attempting to perform.	<ul><li>Put the stones back in the hot water; place the lid on the heating unit.</li><li>It will take about four minutes for the stones to reheat.</li><li>In the meantime find other stones to use, or work a different part of the body until the stones are ready.</li></ul>

The Problem	The Solutions
What if the client gets chilled?	• Keep the client covered at all times. • When doing 'up the left and out the right' (energy flow), you will want to keep your client's hands and feet very warm with fresh stones; exchange these stones often to keep the body warm. • When doing isolated work, cover the body with the towel that is on top of the client and cocoon them with the sheet they are lying on; this helps to lock in the warmth of the stones you have been applying to their body throughout the treatment.
When tucking a stone making sure it is warm and not hot or cool not cold.	• Ask the client 'How is the temperature of the stone?' when you are tucking the stone.
What if the massage room gets hot and humid due to the heating unit and the hot water?	• I have a small fan under the heating unit table; this helps to cool me off. • Open the door between massages.

EXERCISE

Read the full instructions for your heater. Get to know the reset system if the heater has one.

Heat your stones and time how long it takes to get to the required temperature with your own particular system, from hot water and from cold. Place your cool stones in the way you will cool them and then time them.

Well done – you have now worked out what your set-up time can be!

CHAPTER 9

LaStone Therapy
Original Body – the Essence

KEY POINTS

- The energy work in LaStone is the structure of the treatment, the architecture or the skeleton, the very bones.

- The massage or the treatment with the stones is the flesh. One cannot live without the other; they thrive together.

- You will eventually be able to use the stones and the energy work that is LaStone in any therapy you are qualified to practise.

- LaStone therapy uses very specific elements and techniques:

Five element theory	Spinal layout	Proper stone placement
Energy flow	Opening spiral	Closing spiral
Honouring breath	Energy connection	Spinal spiral

- Once you master the principles and techniques, the foundations, you can grow however you wish and use any 'treatment' you wish.

- Keep an open mind during your course; this is complementary to everything you stand for, know and believe.

- If you cannot reconcile what we teach with what you currently believe, ask your instructor for help – we want to show you how to enhance not stop or change your knowledge.

- You may feel challenged on the way!

From Mary:

It is agreed that there are hundreds if not thousands of chakras within the body's systems, that the layers of the auric field are endless, reaching into eternity. It is also agreed that there are seven major chakras, as well as seven primary layers of the auric field, better known as the aura. Each layer of the aura is in kinship with a chakra, and is in turn associated with a psychological function of the body.

If we are clear within ourselves and willing, we can be a catalyst, and channel energies for others to accept the gift of healing. When we can stay balanced and clear, we can open channels of self-healing for our clients. All healing comes from within. We, as practitioners, cannot take credit for a client feeling better or even experiencing some level of healing. Step aside from your ego and become a channel through which energy moves.

Adding heated and chilled stones to a Swedish massage enhances the body's ability to process multiple levels of information within all of its systems at a heightened performance level. Swedish massage with heated and chilled stones may cause complications due to contraindications, so it is necessary to know multiple forms of bodywork to practise it.

I think that all massage therapists should learn at least one form of energy work, such as Reiki, Healing Touch, Brugh Joy's work, Crystal Energy Balancing, Reflexology, or Shiatsu, to name just a few. In combination with the stones, the act of moving energy through the body brings clients into a deeper state of meditation or relaxation without taking risks with the client's conditions that need consideration for that day's treatment. By using the stones in conjunction with an energy treatment, the therapist can help the client bring balance back to both the physical and the mental parts of their being, and to their soul. We can create a feeling of well-being, balanced and cradled by Mother Earth, a sense of wholeness that someone may not have felt for some time.

Energy Work

You may arrive at a course with experience of energy work, or you may believe you don't know anything about it.

As soon as you place your hands on any other person, you are doing energy work, whether you are trained or not. In LaStone therapy we give you some energy tools to help your client and some tools to protect yourself. Used with positive intention they will increase the efficacy of your treatment – your inter-action with your client. We also spend quite a bit of time on the energy aspects of the treatment, because this is generally the 'new' stuff to participants of the course. Anyone on the course is a fully qualified bodyworker of some discipline or other. Not everyone has had energy work explained.

We know that it may feel confusing or awkward at first to have a hot or cool stone placed between you and your client, but you are combining massage knowledge you probably already have to get the technique right. We are simply showing you how to transform your own massage stroke into a LaStone stroke.

The Five Element Theory

LaStone is about creating balance within the body. By observing the five ele-ments we can do this, and it will help all clients' needs.

From Mary Nelson:

With my LaStone therapy treatment, I include all the elements of the Earth to amplify the experience for the client and myself during a treatment. Below is a simplified chart of the five element theory. Keep this in mind when you are choosing what temperature to use on any given chakra; it is an important tool in the success of a LaStone treatment.

A brief description of energy flow from Mary Nelson:

All natural elements flow in one direction and synthetic ones flow in the other. It makes sense that we flow with our clients' natural energy rather than against it.

During a LaStone treatment we touch the body and break the touch with it many times – importantly, once the first stone has been placed, the energy connection is made and remains until the last stone leaves upon completion. In order not to disrupt the client by 'appearing' as if from nowhere, we use the simple but effective 'energy flow' pattern. We travel up the left and out of the right.

About a year before the stones came to me in the sauna room, I was experi-menting with different ways in which to honour the client's breath and energy fields. I was fascinated by the idea of energy fields, the aura and the chakras. At that time I was not educated and had not had the ability to study formally the concept of these beliefs and their basis within a treatment. Nonetheless I was enchanted by the idea that we can alter the human body without touching it. So I began to play around on my own, experimenting with hovering over the body and intuitively feeling with my gut what was happening. I was immensely blessed with willing clients on whom to practise what I was being drawn to learn and know more about. As with all gifts from the universe, Spirit sent to me individuals who had bits of information and confirmations supporting my findings and my ability to listen when my guides call to me.

Element	Organ	Bowel	Surface	Opening	Emotion	Mental	Taste	LaStone
Water	Kidney	Bladder	Bones	Ears	Anxious Fearful	Will power	Salty	Basalt stones are lying in hot water. Marble stones may be resting over ice.
Wood	Liver	Gall-bladder	Nerves	Eyes	Irritable Angry	Mental activity	Sour	Spoon to retrieve the basalt stones from the heating unit. Sheets/towels and all laundry.
Fire	Heart Sex Glands	Small intestine	Blood vessels	Tongue	Moody	Intuition Joy Peace	Bitter	A candle burning. Or the heating unit itself.
Earth	Spleen Pancreas	Stomach	Muscles	Mouth	Worried	Ponder	Sweet	The stones.
(Air) Metal	Lungs	Large intestine	Skin	Nose Sinuses	Sad	Sensitive	Spicy	Feather fan. Heating unit.

One of the ways our soul receives and releases energy is up the left side of our body (the receiving, or 'Yin' or 'passive' side) and out of the right side of our body (the releasing, or 'Yang' or 'active' side). Whether the client is lying in the supine or the prone position will determine the way in which I approach the massage table. I therefore strive to always approach the massage table up the left side and out of the right side of the client's body as much as possible – not that my strokes are in this direction, but my intention is to honour the flow of energy coming into and going out of the soul's body.

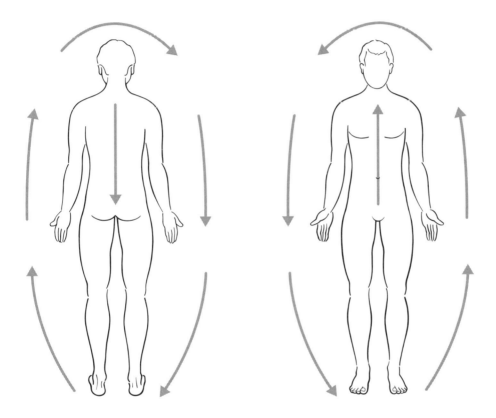

Energy Flow

Honouring Breath

Once you are in the flow, you need to look at honouring your client's breath, their life force. Just as we need to use our breathing to stabilise, centre, ground, and calm ourselves down, and to exert effort, we need to use the breath of our client to work harder and be more effective for them both during and after the treatment.

From Mary:

I cannot stress enough how important breath is. That at all times you must be mindful of the client's breath as well as your own. That breath encourages us to stay in the present moment. It is with and through breath that we can move through life in the body of our choice. To dance with breath, to find the rhythm of breath, to be one with your breath, is to fully be in the now. Breathe and remember this as I explain the piece on the energy connection and its importance in connecting major and minor chakras together in opening spiral, and as you join stones to the body in energy connection.

As you move from one chakra to the next, honour the client's breath, for breath is what allows our soul to stay in body form. Respecting the breath, watch for the rhythm of the client's chest and abdomen. Do they move in unison with each other or is the chest more active in the breath than the abdomen? Is your breath able to match the rhythm of your client's breath and blend as you join the chakra? This joining of your hand with the client's chakra can be physical, with gentle to no pressure, or just above the area of the chakra.

As you match the beat of the breath with your opening of the auric field, separate from a chakra on the inhalation and join the chakra on the exhalation. The rising of the chest/abdomen area is making way for new information to be brought in physically, and the lowering of the chest/abdomen is making room for your hand or a stone to join the body. There is a very small window in which this joining and separating from the body takes place; it is in the fine line between the inhalation and exhalation that this all occurs.

Be mindful and in the present moment as you perform the opening spiral pattern; match the rhythm of the client's breath with yours and above all be focused on your intentions as you open their energy field. In *Joy's Way*, Dr Joy suggests that you hold each chakra for a period of five minutes or more, staying focused in the now. Within a massage treatment or a LaStone session you are blending the opening spiral pattern with massage techniques and the application of heated and chilled stones. In a sixty- or ninety-minute session there is not enough time to hold each chakra for five minutes. I find that staying focused on the opening of the energy field via the opening spiral pattern and moving with this union with each continuous breath you will successfully open the auric field in preparation for stone placement on each of the major chakras when you begin the energy connection.

Spinal Layout

During the LaStone treatment we place stones under and on the body. The spinal layout is the name given to the arrangement of stones we place under the body. The stones used for this will change in size and temperature depending on each individual, but there are some rules to follow.

The stones used for the spinal layout are all found in Bag 1 (*see page 41*). The tools include the following:

- The pillow to be placed under the occipital ridge.
- The twelve spinal layout stones to hug the erector muscle on either side of the spine.
- Two large stones to work the lower back.
- Two sacral placement stones to slide against the gluteus muscle to start deep back work.

Placing your client on the spinal layout means that the treatment starts on their back as soon as they roll down onto the stones. The technique is deeply relaxing and at the same time addresses the main muscles of the spine in preparation for the deeper work once the client is prone.

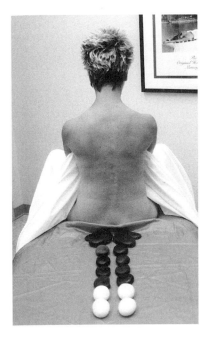 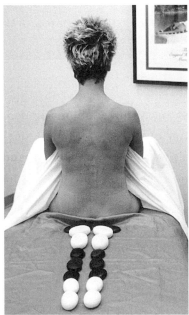 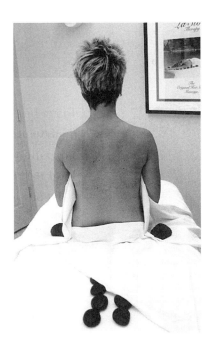

Opening Spirals

In the Greek alphabet, alpha represents the beginning and omega the end.

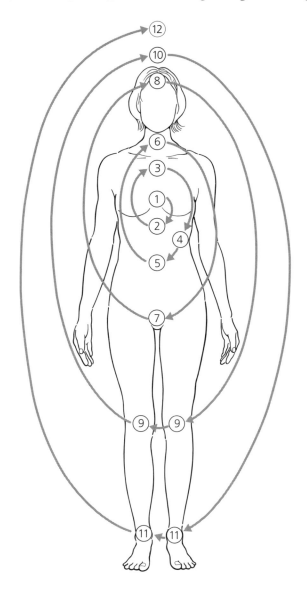

Opening Spiral Pattern (clockwise)

1. Heart – alpha
2. Solar plexus
3. Higher heart
4. Spleen
5. Sacral
6. Throat
7. Root
8. Third eye
9. Knees
10. Crown
11. Feet
12. Transpersonal point – omega

A brief on the opening spiral pattern, from Mary Nelson:

The opening spiral pattern allows the client to experience a profound state of being boundless, a feeling that they are limitless. The borders of their energy fields expand when the opening spiral pattern is done correctly. The opening helps to awaken the chakras and allows for a deeper state of relaxation for the client. This in turn allows for the energy channels to be open and willing to receive healing or light that is channelled to them.

The opening spiral pattern is only performed on the front of the client's body. The front of our body represents the present moment to us, and you can only affect the now – you cannot alter the past. The pattern is always carried out in a clockwise motion over the client's body, starting at the heart centre and ending at the transpersonal point. As you move in a clockwise motion, bow or arch your arm as if you were drawing a half-moon shape from chakra to chakra over the client's body.

It is also important to know that even though you are touching or addressing the major chakras on the front of the body, the purpose of the opening spiral is not to affect or change the direction that a particular chakra is moving in. It is done to expand and clear the auric field. Each chakra is a junction allowing you to move in a clockwise rotation around the body, honouring the breath as you go. Think of the chakra as a door-knob, opening the shutters on the first day of spring and letting in Mother Earth and all her glory.

The pressure of your touch should be that of a 'butterfly' – enough to know that you are there, but not enough to feel the full hand. The position of the hand should be on the body with the palm of the hand flat over the area, except for a few positions: the root, crown and transpersonal point. The position of the hand should be with the ends of the fingers pointing towards the floor. This ensures that the energy is fully 'held' in each position.

Once you have completed the opening spiral pattern, move directly into the energy connection and stone placement, honouring the rhythm of your client's breath as each stone joins the body. At this point you will begin the treatment of choice for this session.

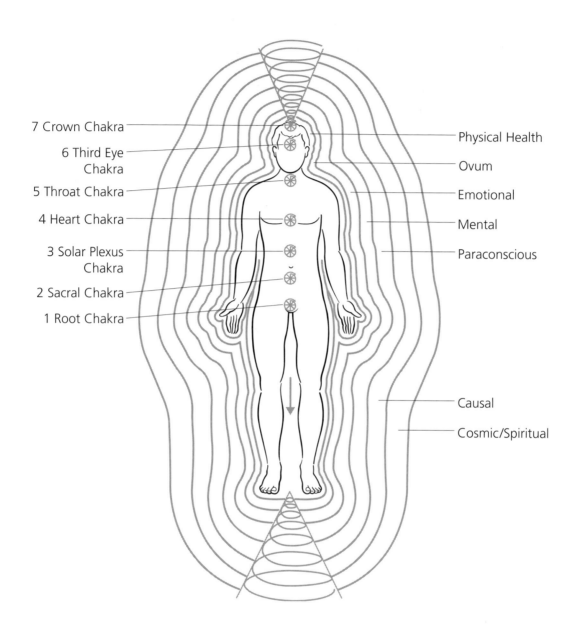

7 Crown Chakra

6 Third Eye Chakra

5 Throat Chakra

4 Heart Chakra

3 Solar Plexus Chakra

2 Sacral Chakra

1 Root Chakra

Physical Health

Ovum

Emotional

Mental

Paraconscious

Causal

Cosmic/Spiritual

Auric Field

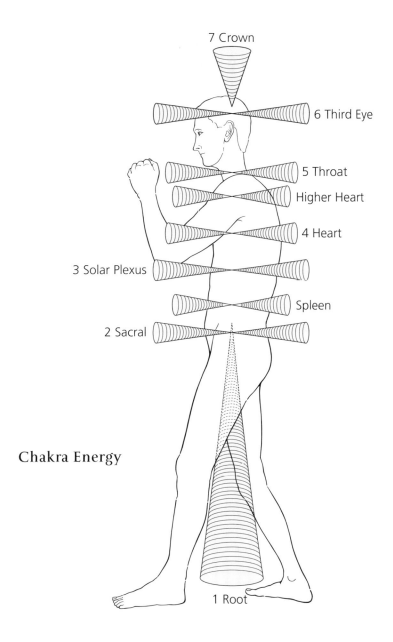

7 Crown

6 Third Eye

5 Throat

Higher Heart

4 Heart

3 Solar Plexus

Spleen

2 Sacral

Chakra Energy

1 Root

Energy Connection

The energy connection can be done on both the present/front/Yin and past/back/Yang sides of the client's body. This technique is designed to bring the chakras in alignment with one another. It is possible, within your energy connection, for you to gently assist the chakra to move in the direction that the body intended it to move naturally. Try using a stone over the chakra, moving it in the direction that flows with the junction the body is taking in that particular area. Then gently place the stone on the body over the chakra with the rhythm of the breath of life.

Energy Connection supine position

While performing the Energy Connection, synchronize your breaths with that of the client and move one hand at a time per each breath – making sure your arms are never crossed, which would block *your own Hara energy*. This energy connection is all about balance; it is vital that you hold two chakras, breathe and allow balance to take place before moving your hand to the next holding position. Please review the Energy Connection stroke sheet carefully and understand it completely; this is high level energy work and will take you and your client to new levels of sensitivity.

Please note that the steps below are expanded beyond the Energy Connection drawings, which are to provide a visual reference of the different holding positions. In the supine position you are standing on the client's right side at all times.

1. Stand on the client's right side.

2. Hold the client's right ankle and right knee and breathe.

3. As the client inhales, move your hand from the knee to the hip near you and breathe.

4. As the client inhales, move your hand from the ankle to the knee near you and breathe.

5. As the client inhales, move your hand from the knee to the client's left ankle and breathe.

6. As the client inhales, move your hand from the hip to the client's left knee and breathe.

7. As the client inhales, move your hand from the knee to the hip on this same leg and breathe.

8. As the client inhales, move your hand from the ankle to the knee on this same leg and breathe.

9. As the client inhales, move your hand from the hip to the hip near you and breathe.

10. As the client inhales, move your hand from knee up to the hip you were just at and breathe.

11. As the client inhales, move your left hand to sacral chakra and breathe.

12. As the client inhales, use your right hand and begin to place the chakra stones on the body in the following order with the rhythm of the client's breath.

13. With your right hand, place a stone in the crevice of the client's left leg and breathe.

14. With your right hand, place a stone in the crevice of the client's right leg and breathe.

15. With your right hand, place the grandfather stone (largest stone) on sacral chakra and breathe.

16. Move your left hand up to spleen chakra as the client inhales and breathe.

17. Pick up a stone with your right hand; place it under your left hand as you roll your hand open to receive this stone, and breathe.

18. Move your left hand up to solar plexus chakra as the client inhales and breathe.

19. Pick up a stone with your right hand; place it under your left hand as you roll your hand open to receive this stone, and breathe.

20. Move your left hand up to heart chakra as the client inhales and breathe.

21. Pick up a stone with your right hand; place it under your left hand as you roll your hand open to receive this stone, and breathe.

22. Move your left hand up to higher heart chakra as the client inhales and breathe.

23. Pick up a stone with your right hand; place it under your left hand as you roll your hand open to receive this stone, and breathe.

24. Hold your left hand over the higher heart chakra stone and move your right hand to the client's right wrist and breathe.

25. Move your left hand to the client's right elbow and breathe.

26. Move your left hand to the client's right shoulder and breathe.

27. Move your right hand to the client's right elbow and breathe.

28. Move your right hand to the client's left wrist and breathe.

29. Move your left hand to the client's left elbow and breathe.

30. Move your left hand to the client's left shoulder and breathe.

31. Move your right hand to the client's left elbow and breathe.

32. Move your left hand to the client's right shoulder and breathe.

33. Move your right hand to the client's left shoulder and breathe.

34. Move your left thumb to client's third eye chakra and breathe.

35. Move your right hand to the client's throat chakra and breathe.

36. With your right hand pick up a third eye stone; place it on third eye chakra and breathe.

37. Move your left hand up to crown chakra as the client inhales and breathe.

38. Move your right hand up to third eye and breathe.

39. Move your left hand beyond the crown to transpersonal point and breathe.

40. Move your right hand to crown chakra and breathe.

41. Move completely into transpersonal point with both hands and breathe.

42. Pause for a bit and allow time to stand still as you breathe in, knowing that by completing this technique you have offered balance and clarity through the stones to your client and yourself.

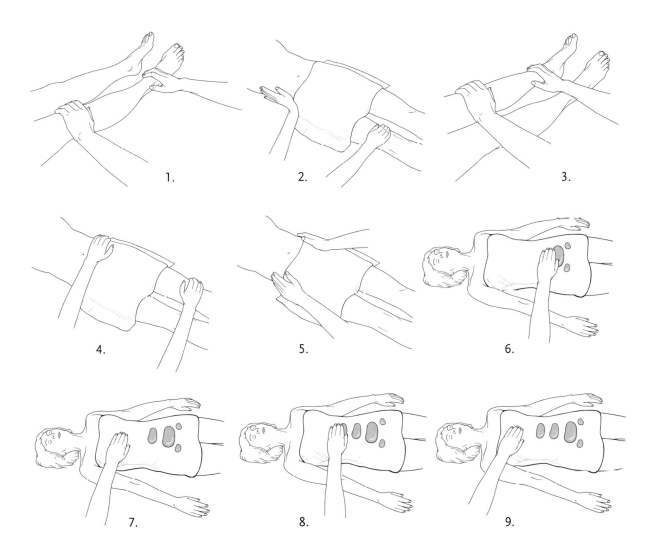

Energy Connection Supine

1. RH – right ankle
   LH – right knee

2. RH – right knee
   LH – right hip

3. RH – left ankle
   LH – left knee

4. RH – left knee
   LH – left hip

5. RH – left hip
   LH – right hip

6. LH – mother hand
   RH – ingual and grand-
   father stones placed

7. LH – mother hand
   RH – place stone

8. LH – mother hand
   RH – place stone

9. LH – mother hand
   RH – place stone

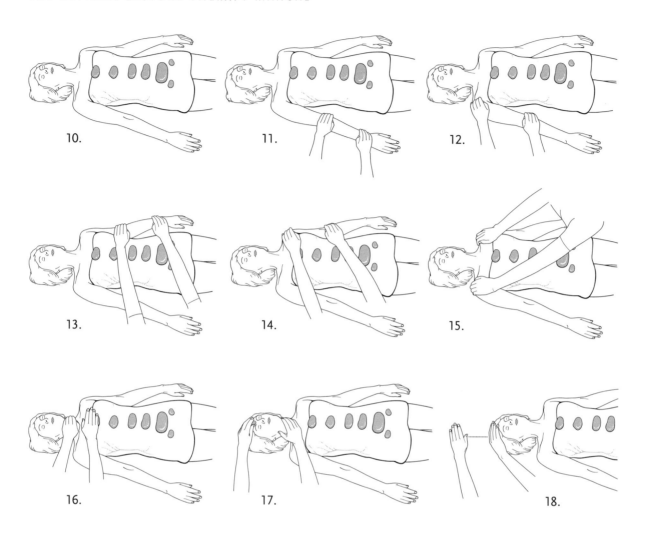

Energy Connection Supine

10. LH – mother hand
    RH – place stone

11. RH – right wrist
    LH – right elbow

12. RH – right elbow
    LH – left shoulder

13. RH – left wrist
    LH – left elbow

14. RH – left hip
    LH – right hip

15. LH – mother hand
    RH – place stone

16. LH – mother hand
    RH – place stone

17. LH – mother hand
    RH – place stone

18. LH – mother hand
    RH – place stone

A brief on the closing spiral pattern, from Mary Nelson:

Once you've completed your work as you were guided to do for this session, finish with the closing spiral pattern.

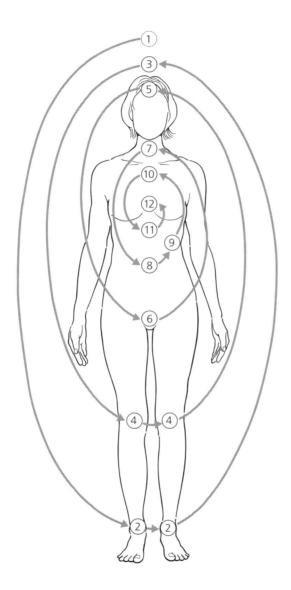

Closing Spiral Pattern (anticlockwise)

1. Transpersonal point	5. Third eye	9. Spleen
2. Feet	6. Root	10. Higher heart
3. Crown	7. Throat	11. Solar plexus
4. Knees	8. Sacral	12. Heart

If left open the client may feel a bit shaky and not quite in their body. The closing brings the auric field back to a normal range of awareness. The closing spiral pattern also seals all that you have just completed so far on the front side/present moment of your client's body, bringing your client back to the present moment with a feeling of renewal, joy and internal peace that will follow them the rest of the day.

The closing spiral pattern is only performed on the front of the client's body. It is always done in an anticlockwise motion over the client's body, starting at the transpersonal point and ending at the heart centre. As you move in an anticlockwise motion, bow or arch your arm as if you were drawing a half-moon shape over the client's body from chakra to chakra (*see page 81*). This is a sealing technique. It quickly locks in all the work you have just completed in the treatment so far. You do not wait for a breath. Moving anticlockwise, infuse love, peace, balance and a sense of wholeness at each chakra, and seal this time reality in your client's heart centre.

After the client has turned over – or if you are working on the prone side only – the energy connection is the starting point.

Energy Connection prone position

While performing the Energy Connection, move one hand at a time per each breath the client takes into their body – making sure your arms are never crossed, blocking *your own Hara energy*.

In the prone position you are standing on the client's left side at all times. Please note that the client's back is fully covered with a towel (not as it appears in the drawings).

1. Stand on the client's left side.

2. Hold client's left ankle and left knee and breathe.

3. As the client inhales, move your hand from the knee to the hip near you and breathe.

4. As the client inhales, move your hand from the ankle to the knee near you and breathe.

5. As the client inhales, move your hand from the knee to the clients' right ankle and breathe.

6. As the client inhales, move your hand from the hip to the client's right knee and breathe.

7. As the client inhales, move your hand from the knee to the hip on this same leg and breathe.

8. As the client inhales, move your hand from the ankle to the knee on this same leg and breathe.

9. As the client inhales, move your hand from the hip to the hip near you and breathe.

10. As the client inhales, move your hand from knee up to the hip you were just at and breathe.

11. As the client inhales, move your left hand to sacrum chakra and breathe.

12. As the client inhales, move your right hand and begin to place the chakra stones on the body in the following order with the rhythm of the client's breath and breathe.

13. With your right hand: place the grandfather stone (largest stone) on sacrum chakra and breathe.

14. Move your left hand up to spleen chakra as the client inhales and breathe.

15. Pick up a stone with your right hand; place it under your left hand as you roll your hand open to receive this stone, and breathe.

16. Move your left hand up to solar plexus chakra as the client inhales and breathe.

17. Pick up a stone with your right hand; place it under your left hand as you roll your hand open to receive this stone, and breathe.

18. Move your left hand up to heart chakra as the client inhales and breathe.

19. Pick up a stone with your right hand; place it under your left hand as you roll your hand open to receive this stone, and breathe.

20. Move your left hand up to higher heart chakra as the client inhales and breathe.

21. Pick up a stone with your right hand; place it under your left hand as you roll your hand open to receive this stone, and breathe.

22. Drape the towel over the higher heart stone to help hold it in place.

23. Hold your left hand over the higher heart chakra stone and move your right hand to the client's left wrist and breathe.

24. Move your left hand to the client's left elbow and breathe.

25. Move your left hand to the client's left shoulder and breathe.

26. Move your right hand to the client's left elbow and breathe.

27. Move your right hand to the client's right wrist and breathe.

28. Move your left hand to the client's right elbow and breathe.

29. Move your left hand to the client's right shoulder and breathe.

30. Move your right hand to the client's right elbow and breathe.

31. Move your left hand to the client's left shoulder and breathe.

32. Move your right hand to the client's right shoulder and breathe.

33. Move your left thumb to client's third eye (back of head) and breathe.

34. Move your right hand to the client's throat and breathe.

35. Place the sock with stones in it behind the client's throat and breathe.

36. Move your left hand up to crown chakra as the client inhales and breathe.

37. Move your right hand up to third eye (back of head) and breathe.

38. Move your left hand beyond the crown to transpersonal point and breathe.

39. Move your right hand to crown chakra and breathe.

40. Move completely into transpersonal point with both hands and breathe.

41. Pause for a bit and allow time to stand still as you breathe in, knowing that by completing this technique you have offered balance and clarity through the stones to your client and yourself.

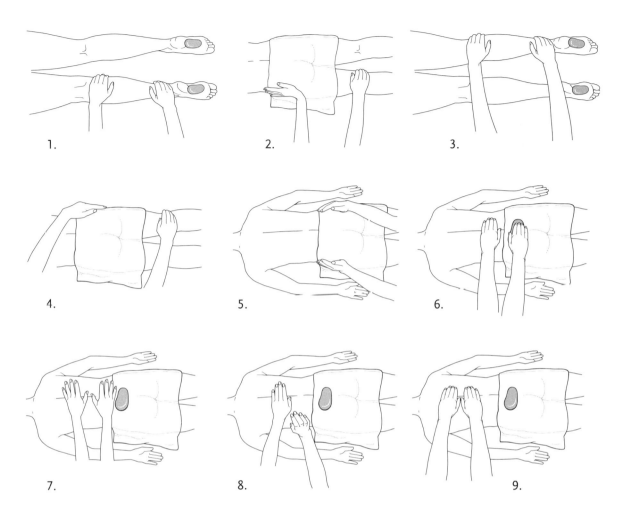

Energy Connection Prone

1. RH – left ankle
   LH – left knee

2. RH – left knee
   LH – left hip

3. RH – right ankle
   LH – right knee

4. RH – right knee
   LH – right hip

5. RH – right hip
   LH – left hip

6. LH – sacral
   RH – place stone

7. LH – solar plexus
   RH – sacral

8. LH – solar plexus
   RH – spleen

9. LH – heart
   RH – solar plexus.

Note that I sometimes place stones on the spine for the back chakras as well (numbers 6 – 9).

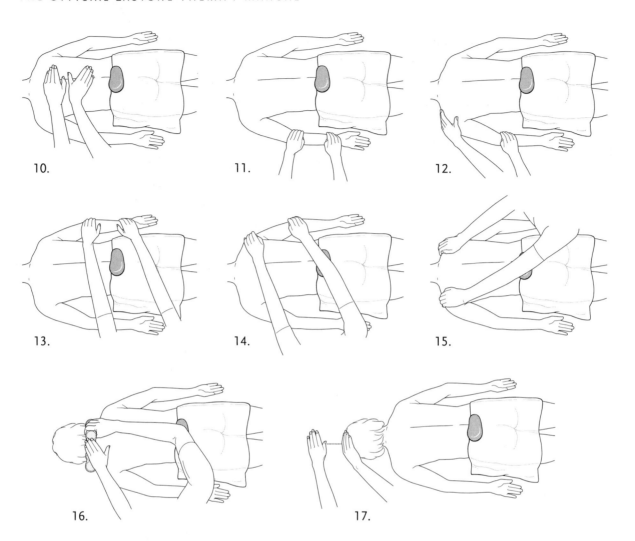

Energy Connection Prone

10. LH – higher heart
    RH – heart

11. RH – left wrist
    LH – left elbow

12. RH – left elbow
    LH – left shoulder

13. RH – right wrist
    LH – right elbow

14. RH – right elbow
    LH – right shoulder

15. RH – right shoulder
    LH – left shoulder

16. LH – throat
    RH – place stones

17. RH – crown
    LH – palm side pointing out

Note that I sometimes place stones on the spine for the back chakras as well.

Now that you are of mind and present with your breath, it is time to bring the stones to the client's body using the energy connection technique. Allow your body to move and dance with this union of breath and Mother Earth's children, the Stone People. As you move up the body from the feet to the legs and torso, breathe and become a part of the experience, the dance of this connection. Pick up a stone and with full intention settle the stone person lovingly on the chakra of choice, then with breath move to the next chakra until you have all the stones on the client's torso. Holding the higher heart centre/chakra and the client's right wrist, pause for a moment. This connection of torso and arm is crucial to allow the body to feel whole. Continue moving up the arms to the throat chakra, the third eye and finish at the transpersonal point, all the time being mindful of breath, the chakras and a small piece of Mother Earth as it joins the body and soul of your client.

Now you are ready to begin the treatment of choice, mixing and exchanging temperatures with the stones. You will be gliding the basalt stone along muscle groups, resting it on or under the body to add warmth, comfort and security. You will be encouraging blockages and inflammation to move through the body with the marble, with its ability to offer refreshment in a time of stress.

The Spinal Spiral

The spinal spiral technique is one that I use to take the client one step deeper into the other world before I finish the day's treatment. This is done with a room temperature stone. Try to find a stone that fits in your hand comfortably and has a bit of a point to it. I use a Chinese fluorite/selenite wand stone. It has been said that this stone helps to aid the balance of the fluid in the spine.

When this technique first came to me I was drawing the circles around the spinous process of each vertebra and then gliding down the length of the nerve that leaves the spine at each vertebra. I was sometimes starting the circles at C-1 and working my way down to the coccyx, and at other times starting at the point of concern for the client's back and working my way up and then back down to the coccyx. I always made sure I drew circles over every vertebra and followed the nerve path from each one.

After a year of experimenting with this concept I met Barbara Hart, a Healing Touch practitioner and instructor. She was surprised when I began to draw circles on her spine and asked me how long I have been working with Brugh Joy's methods. I explained that I had never heard of a Brugh Joy, and asked what a Brugh Joy was. Barbara explained to me who Dr Brugh Joy was and about

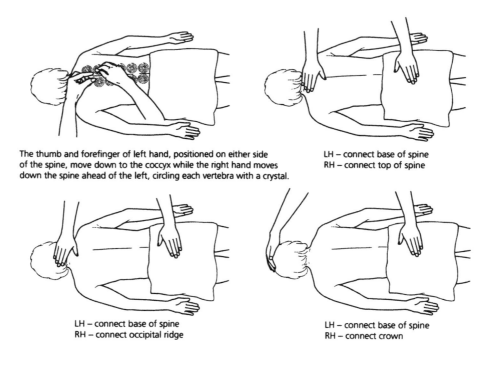

The thumb and forefinger of left hand, positioned on either side of the spine, move down to the coccyx while the right hand moves down the spine ahead of the left, circling each vertebra with a crystal.

LH – connect base of spine
RH – connect top of spine

LH – connect base of spine
RH – connect occipital ridge

LH – connect base of spine
RH – connect crown

Healing Touch, and said that I was already doing much of what Dr Joy has been teaching for over twenty-five years. She encouraged me to begin taking workshops in Healing Touch so I could perfect what I was obliviously channelling in from my spirit guides. It took me another year before I found the means by which to begin my studies with Barbara and the field of Healing Touch. At that point I began to alter and upgrade what I had been integrating about energy work. This truly was the starting point for me to fully begin to realise that I was not crazy and that no one was going to lock me up for what I knew to be true about the body and its energy fields.

Many years later, in 2002, I was honoured to teach at the A.R.E Clinic in Virginia Beach, Virginia. When I demonstrated the spinal spirals one of the students asked me, 'Mary, when did you study Edger Casey's massage techniques?' I replied, 'Never.' To my surprise Mr Casey also spoke about the importance of balancing the spinal fluid with circles along the spinous process, the lamina groove and each of the nerves that leaves the spine, feeding the body on-going information. In Mr Casey's readings he would prescribe techniques that would massage oil blends over the spine by way of drawing circles on or near the spinous process, gliding along the nerve path to extend the oils, allowing the body to physically and emotionally respond to the technique and the oils being used. The order in which the vertebra were approached varied according to the condition of the patient.

This confirmed for me that many years ago when I began to play with this type of technique on the spine I was hearing and responding to my spirit guide – that you do not have to work from C-1 to coccyx, but need to address every single vertebra and nerve that leaves the spine. If you are drawn to begin your spinal spirals in the middle of the back, work your way down to the coccyx, then start at C-1 and bring the whole spine together as one, repeating over the area you began with and ending at the coccyx.

Our ancestors drew on stone to record what they were learning and experiencing in life. The circle clockwise represented Spirit; the circle anticlockwise represented Rebirth. For the first three vertebrae I whisper 'Spirit' when I draw the clockwise circle on the client's right side, gliding down the nerve path. I whisper 'Rebirth' when I draw the anticlockwise circle on the client's left side, gliding down the nerve path. Once you reach the coccyx area maintain your focus on the spine and the fluid within, moving smoothly and effortlessly through the vertebrae, nourishing the nerves and the body. It is now time to seal this work – to do this you need to be standing on the client's right side. As in the case of the closing spiral pattern, the sealing of the spinal spiral technique is essential to the health and well-being of the client's body, mind and soul.

By now you might be asking yourself, 'What is the purpose of the spinal spirals?' I have found that carrying out spinal spirals is one of the fastest ways in which to sedate someone. The vibration of the stone and the circles you create along the spine and nerve endings send everyone into a deep sleep, usually by the time you have done the work on six or seven sets of vertebrae. This is a wonderful technique to use on someone who suffers from sleep deprivation, struggles with relaxation, or has just been in an argument or a stressful situation. If done properly spinal spirals will send your client into never-never land, allowing them to take in all that you have done or will do for them that day.

EXERCISE

Go through the table on page 90 and write in your thoughts or key points to help you.

Rereading the whole section in conjunction with practical application will help you. Remember that you can put all the following techniques together to create a full-body energy treatment. Adding the spinal layout and proper stone placement to your energy connection will make for a fantastic treatment.

Energy Flow
Is up the Yin side (client's left side) and out of the Yang side (client's right side). Yin is the receiving side and Yang is the releasing side.

YOUR NOTES: _____

_____

_____

Opening Spiral Pattern
The opening spiral is the alpha of a LaStone treatment. It is performed on the Yin side of the body only and is done slowly with the client's breath. Think of a fairy wand casting an opening spell – from the heart to the head, clockwise.

YOUR NOTES: _____

_____

_____

Energy Connection
This follows the opening spiral, and should be performed on both the Yin and the Yang sides of the client's body. The energy connection is done with honour – with respect for the client's breath, the Stone People and Mother Earth.

YOUR NOTES: _____

_____

_____

Closing Spiral Pattern
The closing spiral is the omega of a LaStone treatment. It is performed on the Yin side of the body only and is done quickly (not waiting on breath to move through this technique), in order to seal the massage into the client's heart centre.

YOUR NOTES: _____

_____

_____

Spinal Spirals
These are designed to enhance any treatment you offer your client, encouraging their nervous system to respond positively to your touch, the vibration of the stone and the present moment of peace and tranquillity.

YOUR NOTES: _____

_____

_____

CHAKRA AND ENDOCRINE SYSTEM

Chakra	Location	Colour	Gland/organ	Purpose
No. 7, Crown	Top of head. This chakra points towards the heavens. It is positioned in a vertical direction.	Violet-white	Pineal gland	Provides inspiration, wisdom and the understanding of our higher self.
No. 6, Third eye	Between and just above the eyebrows. It is horizontal from the body.	Indigo	Pituitary gland	Stimulates the imagination and increases intuitiveness.
No. 5, Throat	Centre of base of throat. It is horizontal from the body.	Blue	Thyroid gland	Increases vibration, communication and self-expression.
No. 4, Heart	Centre of the chest. It is horizontal from the body.	Green	Thymus gland	Provides forgiveness, compassion and understanding balance.
No. 3, Solar plexus	Above the navel. It is horizontal from the body.	Yellow	Pancreas	Helps with issues concerning personal power, self-control, and letting go of the ego.
No. 2, Sacral (navel)	Below the navel. It is horizontal from the body.	Orange	Gonads	Aids in giving and receiving; building trust in relationships.
No. 1, Root	Base of the spine. It is positioned in a vertical direction.	Red	Adrenal glands	Helps us to achieve success in the material world and the physical body. It is our connection to our ancestors.

For more information, refer to Barbara Ann Brennan's book, *Hands of Light* (*see* Further Reading, *page 184*).

Wheels of motion are here within our bodies, as well as in Mother Earth's body (*see page 74*). The word chakra is a Sanskrit word meaning 'wheel of light'. You, the Earth, and all living things, even the smallest molecules and atoms, are all in motion. The wheels of motion usually move clockwise, although sometimes it can be anticlockwise. I see this movement within our system as being rather like the 'roundabouts' in Britain – every part of our body that joins another part of our body creates a roundabout of energy. Forces of movement come together to create junctions for organs, blood vessels, lymphatic vessels, nerve fibres, connective tissue, muscles/bones and much more.

Example: the brachial plexus chakra. The ventral ramus leaves the body of the vertebra and joins the brachial plexus, which in turn becomes different groups of nerves that feed into our shoulders and arms. At each junction where these nerves join one another a chakra is created due to the movement of energy that is required to sustain this connection. By examining how these roads of nerves come together and leave one another, you can determine the direction in which the chakra flows – whether is it clockwise or anticlockwise. Understanding the flow of energy required at this junction, it stands to reason that when the brachial plexus nerves leave the right side of the client's spine, the brachial plexus chakra is rotating clockwise, and when they leave the left side of the client's spine, it is rotating anticlockwise. Keep this example in mind when you begin to understand the procedures involved in performing the spinal spiral and why the chakra direction is so important.

Once the stones came into my life, the development of what I had been playing around with in energy work rapidly improved. During this time I modified the opening spiral pattern, energy connection, spinal spirals and piezoelectric effect, and the blending of hot and cold stones on the body. I had been incorporating the stones and my form of energy work into LaStone sessions for two years before I began to actually partake in workshops that would increase my knowledge and use of energy within a treatment. It was in my first two levels of Healing Touch that I learned about Brugh Joy and his book *Joy's Way*. I highly recommend this book to anyone drawn to use energy work on their clients. Dr Joy's intuitions are invaluable and will provide you with abundant insight into the energy concepts we as therapists work with on a daily basis. Even if you don't fully understand the composition of the energy fields, you will still be affecting them.

After this, what was coming through to me in my meditations with the stones/energy work, and what Dr Joy had brought to our awareness in the early 1970s, was clear to me. I then began experimenting with a modified form of Dr

Joy's opening spiral pattern (*see page 72*). If you choose to start with the opening spiral pattern you must also end with the closing spiral pattern, on the supine side of the body.

There are many different views on how the energy centres of the body work in regards to releasing and receiving energy. I have been practicing various different forms of energy work for over 17 years and have now come to my own understanding of how the body chooses to receive and release energy. As this understanding became clear in my mind I needed to find a way to help my students embrace this fact. This was easy to find once I began teaching abdominal massage in the LaStone Advance courses.

Our digestive system works to produce energy and release waste from our body. Looking at the flow of the large intestine from the practitioner/therapist's view point you can see that energy moves up the ascending colon on the right side of the body, over the transfer colon and down the descending colon on the left. Therefore releasing unwanted energies from the body is clockwise and bringing wanted energies into the body is anticlockwise.

The chakras in the body all move in a clockwise direction if they are releasing energies and in an anticlockwise direction if they are receiving energies into the body. To bring complete balance into the major chakra system it is important that they all move in opposite directions to each other, creating balance of releasing and receiving as you travel up the chakra system from root chakra up to transpersonal point above to the crown chakra. This alternating of releasing and receiving of energy creates a balanced figure '8' within the chakra system.

To take this concept one step further, I also believe that at any given time my major chakra system can be speaking/releasing energies to Creator – my transpersonal point chakra will be spinning upwards to heaven (releasing) and my root chakra is receiving energies from Mother Earth. All the rest of my major chakras will follow, spinning clockwise, then anticlockwise in turn, maintaining complete balance within my chakra system, thus creating the figure '8' and supporting my whole body from the Earth to the Heavens. This can shift as I need it to shift and the chakras can all spin in the reverse direction. The goal is that all the major chakras between transpersonal point and root chakra are spinning opposite of one another in order to bring balance and harmony to the body.

CHAPTER 10

The Treatment and Techniques

- There are nine rules in LaStone therapy (*see below*). Trust in them and follow them to the letter. Also bear in mind that one stroke with a stone is equivalent to ten with your hands – the temperature is there, so use it, and don't spend your time trying to generate what you already have.

Heated Application

1. Introduce the heated stones to the body with the backs of your hands, demonstrating honour and respect for the stones and the client receiving the temperature.

2. Apply firm pressure with continuous movement to prevent burning the client.

3. Flip the stones every few seconds to prevent burning yourself and offer the warmest side of each stone to the client's body.

Chilled Application

4. Hover the chilled stone above the isolated area of the body that needs consideration.

5. Ask the client to 'breathe', apply firm pressure with no movement, hold and wait for another breath or two.

6. Flip the stones and hold and wait for another breath or two. Then you can begin to move in an isolated area that is requiring the reduction of inflammation, congestion or blockages within the systems of the body.

Geothermotherapy

7. The use of heated stones.

8. The use of chilled stones.

9. The application of alternating temperatures via stones, to bring about a chemical response within all systems of the body.

Massage with the stones, from Mary:

Massage is an art that affects our mental, spiritual, emotional and physical being. We not only massage muscle and skin, but also affect every other aspect of the client with our touch. I feel it is the therapist's responsibility to be centred and clear in order to allow energies to flow through, so that the clients who are open to this type of bodywork will be able to receive the gifts of healing.

Listen to the music as you massage your client, dance with the stones as your hands move over and around each muscle. Slow down for the curves of the body; let the person feel their whole body as one. Glide to the music from the foot, our grounding point, up the left leg of support and reception, over the tension and strength in the back, and out of the right leg of sharing and release. Think about the client's spirit while dancing with them in a massage using stones. The stones come from Mother Earth, just as we do. Our energies are very similar, and the stones have been and will always be willing to aid humans in healing memories as well as in alleviating blocked pain in the physical body.

I usually start a massage with the client in the supine position. Resting the client on the stones, so that they are positioned along the back, first helps to soften and open up the back, which in turn makes the job of the massage therapist easier. I would like you to keep in mind as you read the examples of the stroke sheets (*see page 150*) that they are not only strokes but also examples of the dance with the stones. LaStone therapy is not so much about massage strokes, but about respect and ritual shown to Mother Earth, the Stone People, the client's breath, ceremony and the rhythm of life.

The Techniques and Layouts

These are described here both verbally and pictorially. You may wish to concentrate on some basic techniques at first. This will help you to build your confidence and feel more able with the stones.

Effleurage, petrissage, trigger-point work and tucking will get you off to a good start. As soon as you feel ready to move on, try any of the techniques described below, but most importantly, see how you can convert any of your current massage strokes into a LaStone stroke. Look at where the effort and pressure is in your traditional stroke, slide a stone into that point between the hand and the client's body and see how easily you can transform, turbo charge and perfect your technique. It really is that simple – use the nine rules to guide you and then just play!

Petrissage involves the kneading, lifting and squeezing of the muscles in a rhythmical pattern. This stroke is best done without the use of stones, since petrissage often causes stones to fall to the floor, an unpleasant experience for both the client and the stones. Use petrissage often in your massage to find those deep trigger points or tense muscles, then select the stones you want to use on those areas and use a different stroke to address the problem area.

Trigger-point work applies direct pressure to an isolated area for thirty to ninety seconds (or less if the trigger point releases early). This technique contains many advantages, not only to the client but also to the therapist's body mechanics. Using a warm (not heated) or chilled stone, find the trigger point (you may need to ask the client for help here). Apply deep, firm pressure on the area of need, maintaining constant pressure for up to ninety seconds if necessary.

The warmth/coolness of the stone and the pressure on the trigger point will assist the muscle in relaxing and giving up the knot it has been holding on to, possibly for years – the results are amazing. There is no strain on the therapist's thumbs and wrists and therefore no tension in your own hands while you help your client to feel better. Remember that while you are holding a warm or cool stone your hands and wrists are also healing from the vibration and temperatures of the stones.

When doing trigger-point work on a client through their clothes, make sure you yourself can withstand the heat of the stone – the stone needs to be heated (or very chilled) to allow the temperature to penetrate the clothing, so that the client's muscles will benefit. To hold a stone at such an extreme temperature, I put it halfway into a baby's sock. This acts like a pot-holder. (This is also the way in which I use heated and chilled stones in chair massage.)

Tucking the stones is a distinct way of using the warmth/coolness of the stones to do extra work for you when you are busy working somewhere else on a client. Just slip warm or cool stones under the client wherever specific work is needed. This will heat or reduce inflammation in the area for you in advance, so when the time comes for you to work that area it will be ready and willing for release work.

After you use a set of stones for a certain job on the body, tuck the still-warm or cool stones under an area of tension (*see page 103*). After that, deeper work can take place if need be due to the added vibration and temperatures the stones offered to the body in this tucking action. Sometimes tucking the stones relaxes the muscle to such an extent that the tension just melts away, and your work is done for you. Remember each stone you use when tucking. If you need that particular stone later you may not choose to tuck it; instead, you might want to retrieve another stone from the heating or chilling unit for tucking.

The LaStone Original Body Techniques

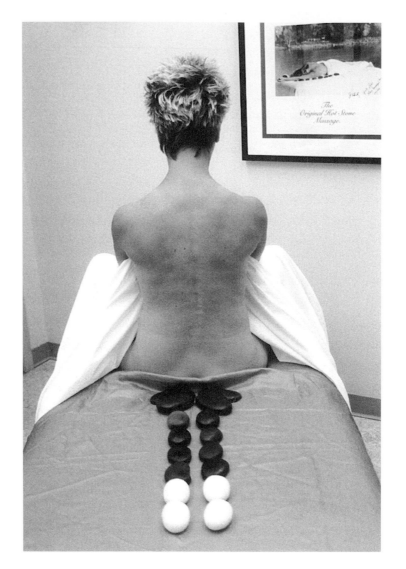

Spinal Layout 1

With heated and chilled stones, large flat and thin stones at the base, moving up in size until the smaller, thinner stones are at the top. Place your stones to accommodate your client's spine.

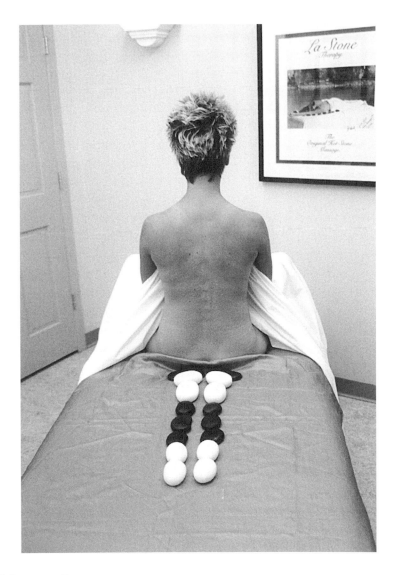

Spinal Layout 2

With heated and chilled stones. Experiment with temperature. Refer to the case notes, think about your geothermotherapy and place your temperature.

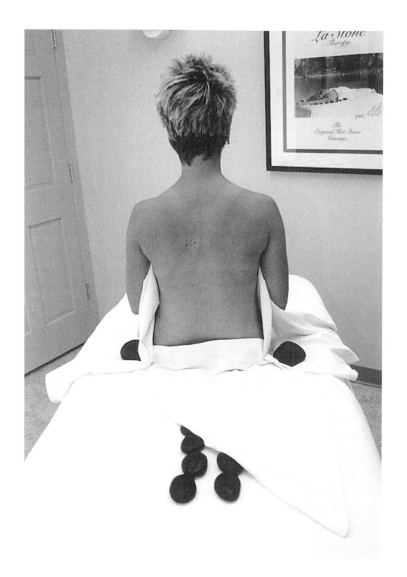

Spinal Layout 3

Covering the stones. Always cover the heated stones with layers of fabric. The stones remain in one place for a while and must not burn your client, who should enjoy the treatment not endure it.

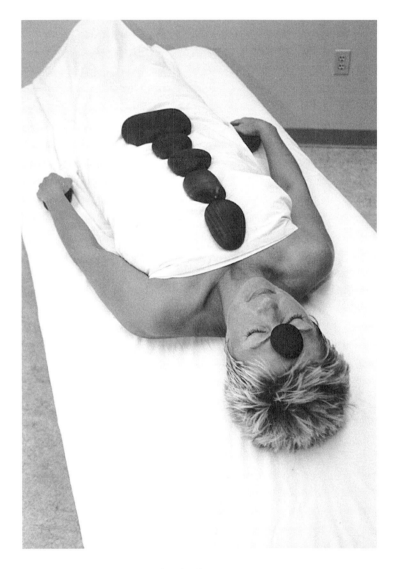

Supine Position with Heated Chakra Stones

Placing stones on the centre line of the client with temperatures that comple-
ment the temperatures of the stones used on the spinal layout enables the client
to achieve deep relaxation within minutes of the treatment starting. Remember:
the temperature and the stones do the work.

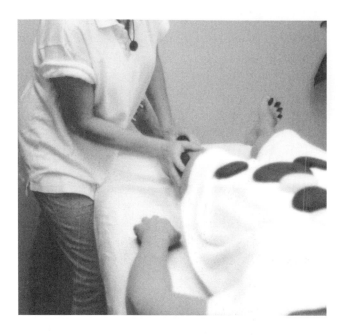

Supine Position: Massaging Anterior Leg

Uncover the area you wish to work, oil it, then using the stones massage firmly and deeply, flipping the stones to share the heat.

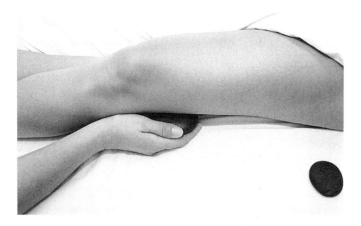

Supine Position: Tucking Stones

Massage with a stone when it is freshly heated or chilled, then tuck it when it is warm or cool. If you have worked a stone until it is no longer in the least bit heated or chilled, place it back in the tank for reheating or cooling. Tucking a neutral stone can be uncomfortable. Tucking stones that still maintain a little of their temperature is like giving your client little gifts throughout their treatment.

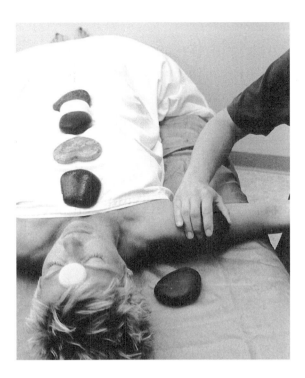

Supine Position: Massaging Anterior Arm with Stones

You can still move the limbs, just as you might do in your current bodywork, and then apply the stones. Remember to support the joints so they are not under pressure, then just sink the temperature in. Firm and deep: delicious.

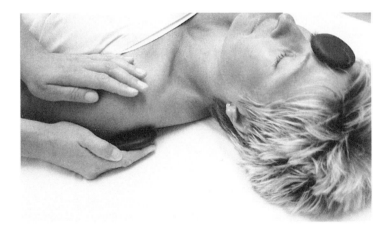

Supine Position: Tucking Stones

Work a stone when it is heated, tuck it when it is warm and return it to the heating unit for reheating when it has cooled.

Supine Position: Alternating Temperatures with the Stones

Alternate temperature anywhere on the body. Every client is different and every client likes different things. Experiment with temperature. Observe the nine rules and help your client to heal.

Supine Position: Massaging the Hands with a (left) Warm or (right) Cool Stone

Pressure-point work, accupressure, reflex work and meridian work – everything is possible with a stone in your hand.

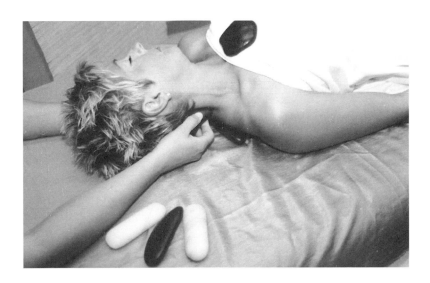

Supine Position: Massaging the Neck Area with Stones Having Alternating Temperatures

The pillow stone has done most of the preparation; just choose a worker stone and use it to do all the work your thumbs and fingers used to do. Hold on trigger points and work that neck nice and deep. Tuck the warm stone and move on to the next one. The tension melts away.

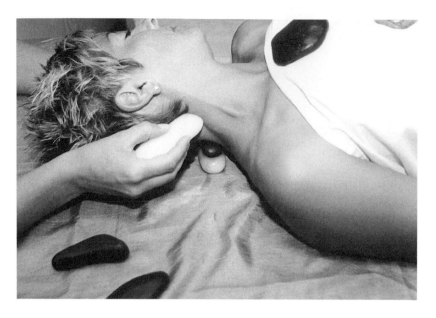

Supine Position: Massaging the Neck Area with Chilled Stones

Finish with a cool stone to go even deeper and make sure all those toxins have 'flushed' through the system.

Supine Position: Massaging the Face with Stones

Face massage with the stones is simply amazing. We dare your client not to drift off to another world.

Supine Position: Resting Stones on the Orbits

Bridge the stones over the eyes, but do not allow them to rest on the eyes.

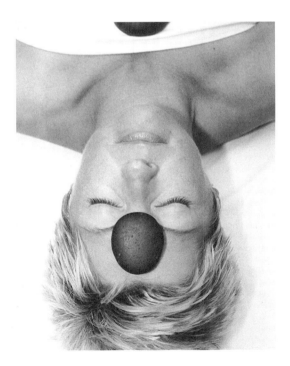

Supine Position: Third Eye Stone

Shown here with a warm stone, chilled third eye stones are great for headaches.

Prone Position: Stone for Belly

The pillowcase covers the belly stone before the client lies down on the stone. Simply folding the pillowcase in half and then over the stone will provide the two protective layers that are ideal for heated stones. Chilled stones can have two, one or no layers – experiment to see which number of layers works the best.

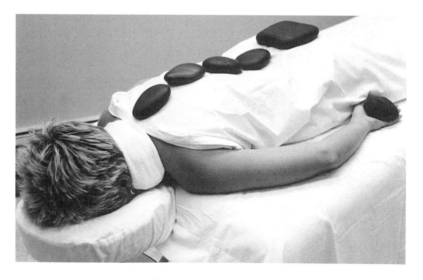

Prone Position: Stones on Back Chakras and Hand Stones (warm)

Once you start to work with the stones you will see that you can place a stone just wherever it will stay. Place the stones in preparation for later work, place them for energy or just simply place them wherever feels right.

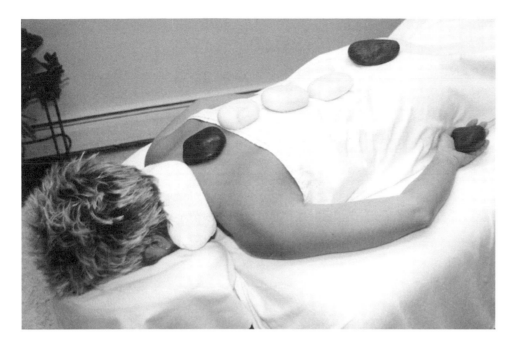

Prone Position: Stones on Back Chakras and Hand Stones (cool)

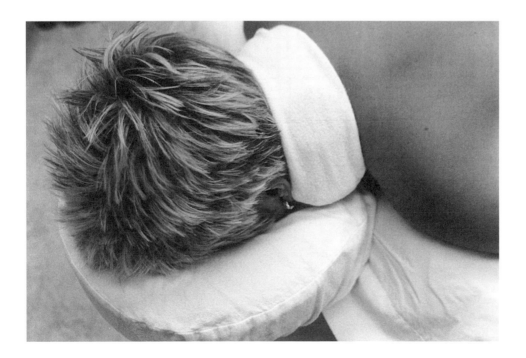

Prone Position: Stones on Back of Neck in a Sock

This is an innovative way to use a pillow stone in the prone position.

109

Massaging with Stones on the Back

Try to have your hand in a 'massage stroke' position. Simply slide a stone between your hand and your client and apply firm pressure. This saves your hands, works deeper and firmer for your client and is familiar to you as a therapist.

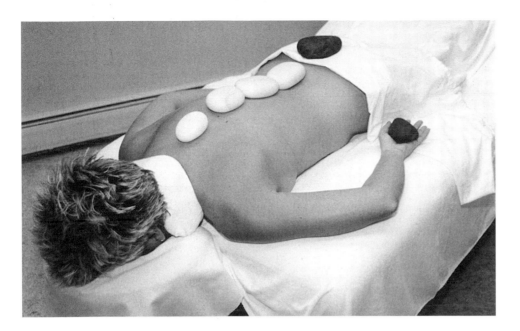

Cool Stones on the Back

Place cool stones along the spine once they are no longer chilled. Work them as the nine rules describe and then leave them on the body to keep the work going while you move on to the next stone and the next stroke.

Basalt Stone in the Hand

Holding hands is comforting, happy, warming, friendly, secure, pleasant, maternal, nurturing . . . holding a stone is all that and more. Your client will not want to let go.

Basalt Stone on the Foot

It's like strolling on pebbles on a beach, warmed by the sun; like taking your shoes off and walking in the grass, letting the sand move between your toes, connecting with Mother Earth. Plug in the heat.

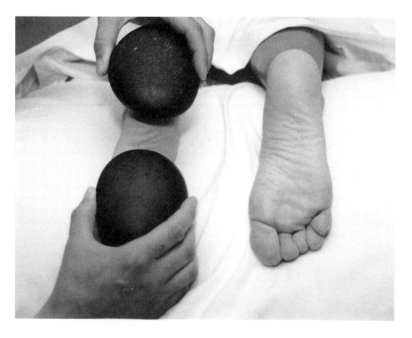

Exchanging Basalt Stones on the Foot to Maintain Temperature

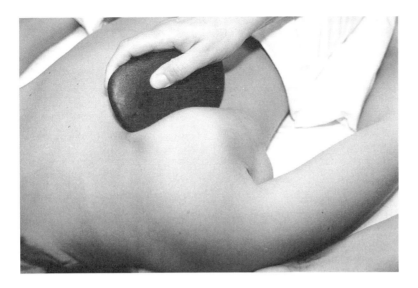

Massaging with Thin Large Stones (warm)

The use of heated stones in this area softens the muscles and allows for deeper penetration. Using a warm stone releases the tension.

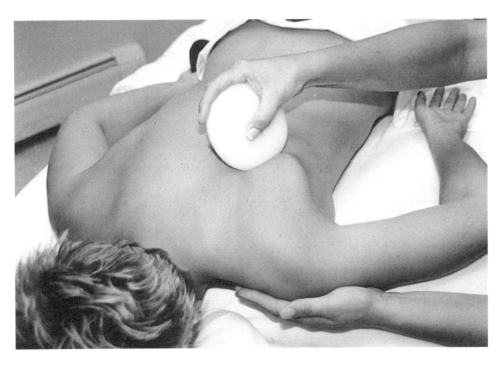

Massaging with Thin Large Stones (cool)

The use of chilled stones in this area speeds up the release of inflammation.

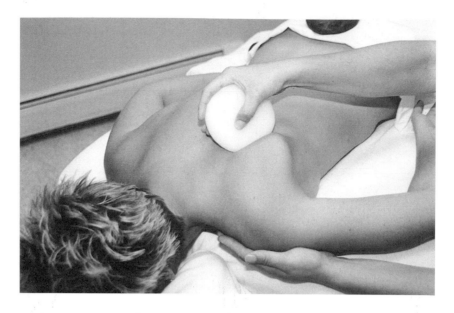

Massaging Deeper with Thin Large Stones

Massaging the Neck Area

The use of heated stones in this area softens the muscles and allows for deeper penetration. The worker stones are great for this area – remember to prepare the muscles with the pillow stone in the supine position and then the stone in the sock in the prone position.

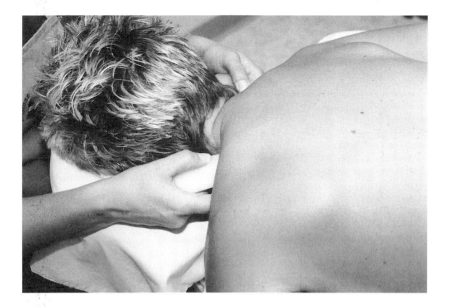

Massaging the Neck Area – Using Chilled Stones

The use of chilled stones in this area speeds up the release of inflammation.

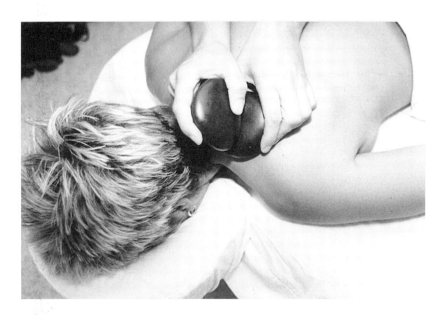

Piezoelectric Effect on the Upper Trapezins

The use of heated stones in this area softens the muscles and allows for deeper penetration. Use sardonyx stones.

Bud technique

This is a Yang experience for the client. The extreme temperatures over bare skin demand that the body, mind and nervous system stand up and pay attention. The concept for this treatment is credited to Bud Fisher from Rochester, Minnesota.

Hold a chilled stone in your left hand and a heated stone in your right hand. The left hand (holding the chilled stone) leads and the right hand (with the heated stone) follows. Starting at the left ankle glide up the left leg and continue up the back just lateral to the spine (the bladder meridian) and off the left shoulder. Walk around the head and continue the application with the chilled stone leading. Apply the stones at the right shoulder gliding down the right side lateral to the spine, then in a straight line off the right leg. This is a revulsive procedure.

Note: if the heated stones are too hot to enable you to move in a straight line without flipping them, you may flip the stones in the air as you travel around the head and/or feet; this flipping action must happen off the client's body. It is just as important that the chilled stone does not lie flat over the organ area of the back. Place the chilled stone on its side while travelling up and down the spine, avoiding organs in the back region.

Cat pawing

This is as close to petrissage as you can get using the stones. Cat pawing is done by holding the stones flat or on their side or ends while you cat paw them back and forth. This method reminds me of a cat pawing at something while purring. Apply firm pressure with this stroke on large groups of muscles. Remember to use warm stones, not ones that are too hot – in the latter case you and your client will not find comfort in the stroke.

Cross-fibre friction

This is deep friction applied across the muscle fibre instead of along the length of the muscle. It aids in breaking up adhesions between the muscles and the skin. Follow the method for friction, below, except go across, not along, the fibre of the muscle.

Friction – chilled

Chilled friction is accomplished by employing light pressure with fast movements over full arms, or full legs, the chest or the back. Applying chilled friction to the body with chilled stones is very effective in stimulating the heart, lungs and lymph system (see page 120 and pages 143–145 for further information).

Friction – heated

Heated friction is applied by using the quick movement of the thumbs or palms of the hands to create added heat, permitting the therapist to work at a deeper level along the length of the muscles. Holding heated stones in your hands will enable this to be accomplished in less time and the heat will last longer. Always remember to keep the stones moving when they are heated.

Holding

This treatment allows Yin energy to penetrate the client's body-mind-soul. The energy generated by the treatment usually becomes evident when there is an increase in heat moving around the area being held. Holding requires that you hold the stones still in an isolated area until you can feel a movement take place. Then release the energy by removing the stones. Place the stones back in the heating or chilling unit as you remove them so that they may return to the temperature they are designed for. One of the first things we remember as children is to hold ourselves after we've been injured, to apply our own energy to stop the pain. As therapists, we can choose to remember this beautiful gift of light we were all given at birth. In turn we can pass on this energy to our clients, to enable them to channel their own tension and stress so as to release what is no longer desired in their body.

Piezoelectric effect

Pronounced pea-aye-zo-electric, this is a rhythmic tapping together of two stones or crystals to create a resonance of sound waves, a flash resonance of light and a burst of electricity into or over the body for deep penetration into the muscles, bones and nervous system. The piezoelectric effect is usually performed by rhythmically tapping together two quartz crystals to create sound waves.

The crystals in quartz are in line with one another, and this creates poles, which in turn can generate the electricity that occurs when the two stones are struck together. The basalt stones are made up of unsorted crystals with many poles going in many directions. It has been my experience with this technique that the nervous system responds to the tapping in a dramatic way not only over the body, but directly on points of tension as well. Clients repeatedly respond to this tapping by saying, for example: 'What was that?' 'I like that,' 'My muscles seem to have relaxed,' 'The knot is less tense.'

To release a stubborn trigger point, use two warm stones. Firmly place one stone (the chisel) on its end for specific work or flat for broad work over the trigger point. Take the second stone (the hammer) and hold it on its end as well, then begin tapping firmly on the stone that is resting on the trigger point. Maintain a constant deep pressure into the muscle with the stone (chisel) while tapping with the other stone that you are using as a hammer. In the event that you are not moving the stone (chisel), it needs to be as warm as you can hold firmly, but not so warm as to burn the client. The stone will seem warmer to the client than to you if it is not moving. Ask for feedback often. Make sure you are working on the trigger point, and be careful not to burn the client. For tapping the stones above the body for releasing negative energy in the aura, the temperature of the stones makes no difference (*see page 41*).

The piezoelectric effect is a powerful treatment. It is very effective if done right before you begin to work deeply into trigger points, softening the area for deeper work if need be. You will find as you master this technique that your clients will fully enjoy the rhythm and music the stones create, as well as the action of receiving some level of healing consisting of blockages/knots in the muscles being eased.

Note: If you want to use chilled stones for the piezoelectric effect, chill two basalt stones. Attempting to do tapping with the marble sardonyx, jade and or quartz stones may, and most likely will, crack your stones.

Rocking the stones

This is done back and forth on the muscle while asserting firm to deep pressure, and results in something of a cross-fibre friction stroke. This aids in breaking down scar tissue as well as tight or knotted muscles. It is done very slowly. Note that the sardonyx balls work very well for this technique.

Stripping

This is a slow, gliding, very intense stroke that follows the length of a muscle or group of muscles from origin to insertion. To do this stroke correctly, the stones must be warm, not heated. One stone is best for stripping. Incorporating piezo-electric effect (*see above*) with this stroke, before or after the stripping, aids in an even deeper release of tense muscles (*see page 114*).

Toning

Use this treatment when you are drawn to help your client on a more profound level. To start, hold two stones of your choice, breathe, and as you feel the resonance of sound coming from deep within your own diaphragm allow those sounds to emanate from your mouth. When you feel the need to remove the stones, do so. Move to the next set of stones. Continue doing this until all the stones have been removed. Remember to place the stones in the heated water or in the ice chest as you remove them.

Vibration

This involves holding firmly in one isolated location on the client and evenly pressing up and down, creating a vibration in the muscles. Sometimes therapists have trouble mastering this technique, and one hand or the other may work better. You can hold two stones that are still somewhat warm (or cool) and link your thumbs together using the dominant hand to control the vibration; you will easily master this stroke. Glide along the area over which you have chosen to vibrate. Do not hold the stones in one place if they are still too hot or too cold. Keep them moving. If, however, the stones are warm or cool, you may stay in one spot. If the stones are too hot to hold tightly, do some effleurage until they reach a tolerable temperature.

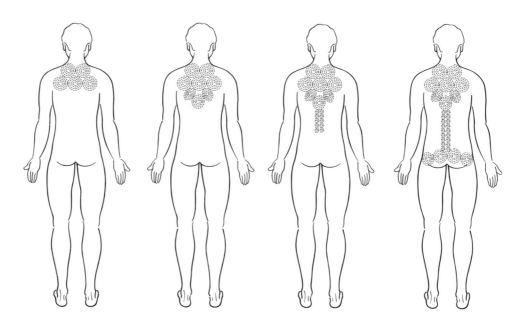

The Four Steps for Applying Chilled Stones, Prone Position

Use very slow, small circular strokes with the stones flat on the upper traps. Use the edges of the stones along the spine at the origin of the latissimus dorsi. You may use the flat side of a stone on the gluteal group and six deep rotators.

Note: *never* initiate hot or cold stones while *massaging* on the latissiumus dorsi as this part of the back protects the liver/anger and kidney/fear. You can begin the massage with either heated or chilled stones along the hip or shoulders and slowly bring them into this area of the back, but do not initiate the extreme temperature while massaging in this area. This rule does not apply to stone placement in the spinal layout.

Home Visits

It is possible to practise LaStone therapy by arranging home visits to clients, although it involves a bit more work not only for the therapist but also for the client. See page 189 for information on what to bring, in addition to what you need to take when going on home visits. I load all my massage items into a large carpet bag I made from upholstery material. The heated stones are placed in the heating unit just as they normally would be, without the water. The chilled stones are placed in an ice chest with ice. This way of packing gives me just four items that I need to bring into the client's home: the carpet bag, the heating unit, the ice chest and the massage table.

At the time you arrange the appointment ask the client if they are willing to have one to two gallons of heated water on their cooker for you when you get there. This will save you twenty to thirty minutes of heating time. Also ask for a small table to set the stones on. The first thing you set up when arriving at the client's place is the heating unit and both the heated and chilled stones. Always, even in your own place of work, place a towel under the heating unit to absorb any water that may drip off as you are pulling stones out. You'll also need to put a towel next to the heating unit to set the stones on, to remove a bit of the heated water before you take the stones over to the massage table and the client. If you take dripping wet stones to the massage table the client may end up lying in a puddle of water, which would not be very pleasant for them, and water on the floor could pose a hazard because it could make the floor slippery.

When the table and stones have been set up, pour the heated water over the stones in the heating unit and turn it on its normal setting to give you your chosen temperature in the range of 110–140°F/43–60°C. Once the stones are heating set up the massage table, the ice chest nearby and all the goodies you will need for the therapy session. By that time, five minutes or so, the heated stones will be ready. You can be set up and ready to go to work in less than ten minutes if the client heats the water for you in advance.

EXERCISE

1. List three different techniques for using a stone.

2. List three different places or times you would tuck a stone.

3. List three different places you would put a stone during a treatment.

Geothermotherapy – 'The Science of the Stones'

> **Disclaimer**
>
> No procedures, treatments, or suggestions of variable temperature and durations of variable temperatures described in this chapter are prescribed. Only a licensed health professional is qualified for such procedures and/or prescriptions. Any suggestions of possible treatment given in this book are purely for personal use.

Contributions

LaStone® instructor Patricia Warne, LMT and Robert Stump, senior analyst, Modern Technologies Corporation, DCSCD, RID/CID, HQ TRADOC.

KEY POINTS

- LaStone therapy is the application of alternating temperatures delivered by natural stones from Mother Earth – geothermotherapy.

- The temperature does the work; the stones deliver the message.

- The simple application of temperature through the placement of stones has all the effects of geothermotherapy.

- Step back and see that trusting the stones does the work.

- Because of the variables of time, temperature and stones, anyone can benefit from LaStone therapy.

- The massage or treatment is the icing on the cake; the therapist is an assistant to the temperature and the stones.

Less Is More

Because the principles of LaStone therapy rest so much on its relationship to temperatures, it is important for you as the therapist to have a working understanding of applying alternating temperatures to the body. Neither heat nor less heat (cold) heals the body; only the body heals itself. Heat and less heat (cold) can increase the body's ability to heal. Throughout this book we refer to the use of heated and chilled temperatures in a number of ways: *hot, heated, heating, heat or less heat, cold and chilled*.

Geothermotherapy is the application of either heated or chilled stone to the body for the purpose of changing the physiological responses within the body to promote healing. During the application of chilled stones the internal body begins to heat itself because the body will always attempt to return to homeostasis.

Circulation is rapidly changed with the practice of geothermotherapy, and if circulation is increased, then so is nutrition and the way that every cell in the body responds to the experience of the alternating temperatures being applied. Circulation is key to health. We go to the gym to increase our circulation, to promote health and well-being. Think of LaStone as a passive workout in the gym. We take our internal organs and systems to the gym while our bodies and minds relax by the pool – free to dream and travel, and returning fully fit.

It is believed that when you increase the blood flow through the skin detoxification is increased, supporting the liver, bowel and kidneys, and the lymphatic and circulation systems. All areas of the body's systems continue to respond for seventy-two hours after a LaStone treatment, during which healing occurs within the body.

When using both heated and chilled stones in a massage, you are accelerating the exchange of blood, lymph and digestive fluids in the body, and increasing the blood flow to the area to which the stones are applied. Isolating chilled/cool stones on an inflamed area will facilitate the removal of toxins and inflammation, encouraging a healing response deep within the body's systems.

As with all modalities that promote a chemical response within the body, caution and the full understanding of the treatment are of key importance. The power of thermal energy – whether it be in the form of heated or chilled stones – requires application to the body by a skilful and knowledgeable therapist. It is therefore important that you take the time to fully grasp the method used to apply alternating temperatures to the body and form a respectful relationship with the power of hot and cold (less heat) philosophies. Just as important, you must overcome any prejudices you may have in regard to the use of cold temperatures in treatment. Without the knowledge and appreciation of heated and chilled temperatures to the body it is near to impossible to become successful in using the stones in LaStone therapy. Temperatures and the practice of alternating temperatures are potent modalities, which must be respected and used to their fullest potentials. Applied improperly they can harm; applied with skill they can promote healing in the individual.

A few thoughts on alternating temperatures: we can create balance by using a balance of temperature. If we choose one temperature alone (usually hot, because we think it feels nice) we eventually tip the scales and leave our client desperately trying to cool down just to get to normal body temperature – basically we 'cook' the client. Would you put your friend or client in a sauna for an hour and expect them to be OK? Definitely not. Now, if you put your friend or client in a sauna and let them come out and have a cool shower whenever they wish, they will have a far better time and their body will be left alone to heal instead of trying to protect itself to survive.

When we get warm it is lovely, but when we get hot we open a window and feel the nice cool breeze – we cool down. Hot and cold are both wonderful at the appropriate times.

> Too much hot is unpleasant and sweaty.
> Too much cold is unpleasant and gives you goose bumps.
> Warm is fab, relaxing, balancing and feels good.
>
> **Hot + Cold** = Warm and balanced

Geothermotherapy: the Basics

The effect of short-term heat on the body is as follows:

- **Causes vasodilation** – a stimulating widening of the blood vessels, increasing blood supply and leading to flushing.

- **Increases circulation** – floods the body with oxygenated blood, highly nutritional fuel.

- **Increases metabolism**, improving the rate at which the body processes foods and toxins, burns energy and clears through.

- **Increases pulse rate**, thereby improving the circulation and helping the heart to pump efficiently.

- **Increase cell metabolism** – the rate at which the body manufactures good chemicals, helping hormones, blood cells and the immune system.

- **Increases lymph function**, putting the body's waste-disposal system on full speed and high efficiency.

- **Decreases the stimulus of the myoneural junction** – this relaxes the muscle response, relaxes the client and allows the therapist to get into those muscles with less discomfort.

- **Reduces spasticity in the muscles**, allowing an increased range of work and reducing tension.

The body becomes deeply relaxed, healing takes place more efficiently and the therapist is able to work more deeply. All the above increase and promote the body's ability to heal itself. Even if massage is not carried out with the stones, as soon as temperature is applied all the above occurs. Trust the temperature.

If you *only used heated stones* in the treatment, it would become a long-term application, which would act in a depressive way on the circulatory system. Simply put, the body would start to think, 'I'm getting a bit hot – instead of relaxing I am going to have to so something about this to try to cool down'. Continued application of heat will result in the body taking up to a third of the blood away from the central organs and brain, to allow cooling, and this will result in the body feeling very tired. It will also result in the stopping of the cleansing, detoxing and processing as the body goes into 'protect and survive' mode.

Your client may mistake this for deep relaxation – they might say something like, 'I couldn't do a thing after the treatment; I was in a daze,' because too much heat will have depleted their body. Dizziness can be caused as blood is moved away from the brain in this cooling process. Heat applied over a long term will cause the body to try to cool down by pumping blood to the outer regions and skin away from core organs to cool down and maintain optimum homeostasis.

The body begins to work on maintaining homeostasis to return to a normal 'safe' state.

So remember, with heat application – less is more!

When applying and leaving a heated stone (placement) to the skin, there will be an instant concentration of blood to the area; if prolonged application occurs then hyperaemia occurs.

The contrasting short-term effects of cold on the body are described below. Note that cold will feel as if it penetrates the muscle more quickly than heat. It will travel rapidly deep into the core, so application may be shorter than the application of heat. See page 145 for a further explanation.

COLD IS USED:

To create perfect balance – Yin to Yang.

In cases of inflammation/pain being present.

In cases where toning is required.

When you have caused excess heat or wish to 'flush' blood and/or muscle.

When cold stones are applied, they remove heat – remember that we use marble slabs to remove excess heat from food and to keep it fresh for longer!

So here is how cold affects the body:

- **Vasoconstriction** – the narrowing of blood vessels, restricting blood supply to different areas of the body.

- **Analgesic effect** – the body releases a natural pain relief substance (prostaglandin), which in turn reduces muscle spindle spacticity. This helps us to work deeper with less pain.

- **'Breathe deeply' effect** of temperature change – increases circulation and oxygenation of blood.

- **Inhibits release of necrosin** – natural chemical that causes arteries and vessels in damaged muscles to clot and starve muscles of blood.

- **Reduces inflammation** – excess blood is sent away from area.

- **Reduces histamine** – the irritant present in stressed muscles – which results in the relaxation of the muscles.

Long-term application of cold stones will cause the body to attempt to maintain homeostasis and this will result in vasodilation – in other words in the sending of large amounts of blood to a cold area to warm it up – *application of both heated and chilled stones thus results in a heat treatment*. Heated and chilled temperature applied alternately also help to balance acidity and alkalinity (pH) in the body.

The aim of a LaStone treatment is to cause a 'rollercoaster' effect by using heated and chilled stones.

Using alternating temperatures:

Heat is applied.

Vasodilation.

Increased metabolism.

Increased pulse rate.

Increased circulation.

Increased cell metabolism.

Increased lymph function.

The body becomes deeply relaxed.

Healing takes place more efficiently.

The body eventually adjusts and homeostasis is reached.

THEN

Cold is applied.

Immediate vasoconstriction.

Sharp intake of breath/oxygenation.

Analgesic effect.

Inhibited release of necrosin.

Reduction of inflammation.

Reduction of histamine.

The body pumps blood to the core organs to keep them warm and eventually adjusts so that homeostasis is reached.

Then heat is applied, etc.

Then cold is applied, etc. . . .

If the application of heated and chilled temperature is rotated during the treatment over ten- to fifteen-minute periods there is a continuous process of vasoconstriction and vasodilation, which results in increased flushing rates within the body and optimum healing.

They do more together than they can ever do apart.

This rollercoaster effect is crucial for the optimum LaStone treatment – the combination of heated and chilled stones provides optimum healing conditions. The client will be relaxed emotionally when receiving the treatment, while physically the body will be doing a heavy 'internal workout', which will ultimately result in the body feeling totally relaxed both physically and emotionally.

Blood Soldiers, as told by Patricia Warne

This story was written by Patricia Warne, to help people to understand the effects of alternating temperature on the body. It is a really useful tool for explaining to your clients what is happening. They need to know what the effects are without the technical details.

Patricia Warne, our hydrotherapy expert, was the second person to join Mary in sharing the magic of the stones with other bodyworkers. Keep in mind while reading this short story that our bodies are factories – that at any given moment in a twenty-four hour period our systems are demanding that our body responds to the internal and external happenings. At times this response needs to be immediate and with appropriate action to cause a change within in our body.

In an effort to explain the effects of temperature on the human body, I have found the 'blood soldiers' analogy to be very effective. It goes like this. Many of the body's systems are dedicated to making sure that the body remains at its temperature of 98.6°F/37°C degrees. There's a balance that needs to be maintained. When that balance is disturbed, the body must go to work to correct itself.

We can look at this in the same way that we look at war. This is something that the human understands, unfortunately. When soldiers are waiting to go to war or to bring in peace, or a balance, where there's been a disturbance, they hang out in the barracks waiting for direction from the commander. The body works in the same manner. You have your brain as the commander-in-chief giving out orders to all the soldiers that live within your body. You have your enzyme soldiers, your immune system soldiers and your blood soldiers, just to name a few. I am going to discuss mainly the blood soldiers. The brain and the body are also equipped with runners or informants, who are in constant communication with the commander about the condition of the body. So let's look at a LaStone treatment

The body enters into this treatment at its normal temperature of 98.6°F/37°C. The massage begins with the application of heated stones. Now heated stones are not such a big threat or an attack to this balance, although the heat given out by the stones is slightly higher than the body's normal temperature. So, your informants run to the commander in a split second and give the information that there's been a change to the periphery, or skin surface. It's not a large change, so not too many troops (blood soldiers) are needed. The commander-in-chief gives the order for the blood vessels to widen slightly, allowing a few more blood soldiers to go to the area. We thus have a slight reddening of the skin and warmth where there are more blood soldiers. The commander-in-chief even donates some of its own blood soldiers, so a slight sedation takes place and everything's cozy warm.

Now, all of a sudden, a hugely different temperature is applied, in the form of the chilled stones. This warrants sending many soldiers to the area to bring the balance back. The informant, in a spilt second, rushes to the commander-in-chief and screams '*attack!*' There's a huge disturbance to all systems. At the sight of the disturbance all the blood soldiers are forced away from the front line, which is the skin. This is known as vasoconstriction. So, for a moment, all the blood soldiers in that area are pushed away from the superficial tissues.

The body perceives this as a threat to its survival and acts accordingly. The commander-in-chief, who's very brilliant, sends out all troops to the area. The troops have been hanging out in their respective places, waiting to be of service. We have the kidneys, the liver, the heart-and-lung centre (the largest of the areas) and all other vital organ systems. The command is given. The front line has been dropped and in defence the commander-in-chief sends in ten times as many troops to the area. They don't stop and ask for directions and plough through everything in their way. They rush to the area in mass quantities, bringing lots of back-up, or blood, to the area that has just been under attack, warming and clearing out all organ and muscle tissue in their path.

This is how a cold application in brief doses actually creates heat. The vital organ system has been cleansed and toned, becoming stronger for having to go to work and rise to the challenge of its disturbed homeostasis. This strengthens the body's immune functions and overall vitality.

Now that the client understands, it is time the therapists had some more information . . .

Geothermotherapy – the Detail

Hydrotherapy and BTUs

Let's get back to the subject of water and the role it plays. As the temperature of the stone (or stones) increases perspiration during a LaStone therapy treatment, the need for increased water becomes mandatory for survival. Water has the highest specific heat of all substances besides ammonia. It is the mother ship of all thermal energy storage materials, on a pound-per-pound basis. It takes one BTU (British Thermal Unit) of energy to raise the temperature of one pound of water by one degree Fahrenheit. Water weighs 62.4 pounds per cubic foot. Stone, on the other hand, does not have the heat capacity of water and can hold only 25 per cent of the heat that water can. Mathematically speaking, stone does not have the heat capacity that water does. So, why do the stones work within a LaStone therapy treatment? Stone weighs 100–150 pounds per cubic foot. Per volume, stone is denser than water, so it makes up in density for what it does not have in specific heat capacity.

The first law of thermodynamics is 'It's all about heat!' There is no such thing as cold – there is only less heat. On another note the body does not absorb cold; it only looses heat. In the maths and science of thermal energy it goes like this.

Energy, or thermal energy in science terms, is classified in two ways, BTUs (British Thermal Units) or watts. These are units of energy. The human body in its resting state displaces 240 BTUs per hour. This is equivalent to a 70-watt light bulb. This is also known as a sensible heat. The body also uses 180 BTUs an hour of what's known as latent heat or moist heat. The body looses one-fifth of a pound of water per hour through latent heat in its resting state. The need for water becomes obvious. With increased activity, use of these energies through perspiration can rise to 900–1000 BTUs per hour. This can result in a loss of one pound of water per hour when the body is in an active state, versus its one-fifth usage in its resting state.

During a LaStone therapy treatment the body is working hard with these simple principles of sensible and latent heat. Sensible or dry heat is what's happening in the spinal layout, the chakra layout or when stones are tucked.

In the case of a LaStone treatment a heated or chilled stone is the message for delivering therapeutic heat. The epidermis and the muscles are the reception of that heated or chilled temperature; the stone is the medium. The application of chilled stones results in a *heat-producing* or *heat-reducing* effect. This is determined by the duration of the temperature applied to the body. Chilled stones receive heat from areas of the body where there is an excess of heat.

Before beginning LaStone therapy you must find out from your client what their needs are for the day. Do they have any recent injures that they are trying to deal with? Is there chronic tension in their daily lives, or both? There is a helpful list of considerations for LaStone therapy on page 140. Do look it over and use whatever part of it applies to the type of therapy sessions you will be offering to your clients while using the stones. It will help you decide on the type of treatment, the placement of temperature and the combination of the stones.

Applications of either heated or chilled stones produce a series of internal responses. Working with temperatures acts as a *derivative*. This decreases the flow of blood and lymph from one area by increasing the flow of blood and lymph to another area. It is important to understand these responses in order to determine the course that a treatment should follow. Two of the main responses are *tonic* and its reverse, *atonic*. If you choose to use heated stones only, end the treatment with a vigorous application of chilled stones to maintain the reaction of toning (*see* Terminology, *page 182*).

Applying/massaging with both short- and then long-term application of chilled therapy is called *active hyperemia*. The superficial constriction of the skin (short term), and the vasodilatation of the skin (long term), relieves congestion and blockages in both the internal organs and the muscle fibres. This can create lasting relief for clients for many days, with the possibility for total alleviation of the congestion, and relief at trigger points or from blocked areas in a client's body.

The primary action of prolonged application of heated stones to a reflex area causes passive dilation of the blood vessels of the related organ. When incorporating LaStone therapy principles in a treatment, it is important for hydrotherapy to be fully understood. The use of heated stones on an isolated area will pull blood from the organ and to the tissue of that region. The result will be warm, flushed skin (hyperemia). This will open doors for you as a therapist to work even deeper on those impenetrable trigger points and tense muscles. Think how hard you normally have to work to get that blood to move when you are doing your traditional massage. LaStone speeds up the process, allowing you to get deeper, and be more effective, sooner.

A prolonged application of heated stones, followed by a brief application of chilled stones, causes dilation and constriction of blood vessels and increases white blood cells in a given area. Alternating between both temperatures in a massage will support your efforts to bring down inflammation and stop congestion in your clients. This makes this treatment invaluable in chronic and acute cases, both for your clients and for you as a massage therapist.

The primary action of the short application of chilled stones to a reflex area causes active dilation of the blood vessels in the related organs. This has an immediate numbing effect, thus reducing the discomfort that accompanies strains, sprains, fractures and contusions, and reducing fluid build-up in body tissues. When chilled stones are used in isolated areas, the body tries to heat itself because the body's internal environment wants to remain relatively constant (homeostasis). Using chilled stones is therefore also a *heating treatment*. The secondary action of the use of chilled stones is to rehabilitate injuries and chronic muscle spasms. The chilled stones help to speed your client's return to normal activity. What is not commonly known is that using chilled stones in a massage increases the range of motion and stimulates muscles and the nervous system.

A Hot Oil Treatment Into the Bargain

The two most important therapeutic agents available to any healer are water and heat in all their variables. The greater percentage of the body is made up of water; it therefore stands to reason that water in all its forms can enable the body to heal itself and maintain balance. The fact that our bodies need to maintain a narrow range in temperature is evidence enough to support the use of heat and less heat (cool) in all its variables to promote healing.

Almost as important as the water is the oil used in a LaStone treatment. Here is a story provided by Dave Pleshek, a small-engine mechanic. It will give you a working understanding of the benefits of oil within a heated treatment.

> . . . The two main functions of motor oil in an engine are to transfer the heat from the engine block to the oil pan or oil cooler, and to lubricate the engine. Without proper oil flow the engine would overheat and seize up. To put that into the context of LaStone therapy, without oil or with insufficient oil the skin is dry, and this works like an insulator. There is a barrier that retards the thermal energy's ability to penetrate into the muscle and tissue. When there is adequate oil and moisture there is better conduction and convection. Therefore when you glide an oiled heated or chilled stone on a body, the oil transfers the energy deeply into the muscle and tissue(s). Conversely, when there isn't enough oil on the body the experience is superficial and the autonomic nervous system (ANS) will be activated. So if deep penetrating heat is your goal you must use oil. If there is a lack of oil the thermal energies are not distributed adequately, so that the temperatures lie on the surface of the skin with little or no benefit to the client's needs and without effectively addressing their underlying problem areas.

Another component and benefit of using oil within a LaStone treatment is the feeling of the smoothness as the stone and oil glide along the curves of the body. A lack of oil will cause the stone to grab at the client's skin rather then glide along each muscle group. The result will be a reaction within the ANS without deep, penetrating heat being transmitted to the areas in need of attention. When the appropriate techniques for using oil and heated stones have been utilised and brought together with Swedish strokes, the client's pores begin to open, allowing the absorption of the oil into the epidermis at a deeper level than without the heat.

The result is a hot oil treatment. It is my recommendation that you choose to use high-quality oil for a LaStone treatment. I prefer Jojoba (HOBACARE, www.bostonjojoba.com) to any other type of oil; it softens the different body hair like no other, does not go rancid, will not stain your sheets and is chemically the closest to our own body's oil.

The Importance of Water in LaStone Therapy

It is essential to encourage your clients to drink water before a LaStone session so as to prepare their body for the removal of unwanted inflammation and toxicity that might be causing some of their discomfort. This intake of water before a geothermotherapy session or any massage treatment is very important for the success of the treatment. When we perform Swedish massage on the body it begins the process of removing toxins from the body. If the kidneys and liver are in short supply of water, the body's filtration system will not be able to get rid of unwanted toxins. Adding temperature to a Swedish massage as we do to a LaStone session demands that the body responds, not only to the modality, i.e. Swedish massage, but also to the increase of blood flow encouraged by the temperatures. If the body is working overtime to process the information of the massage and the temperatures being applied, then the kidneys, liver and all systems of the body will be in desperate need of hydration. The only real way to hydrate the body is with pure water. It is important that the water be of high quality, so it may be necessary for you to offer your clients filtered bottled water.

Doctors are discovering that some individuals are developing an allergic reaction to their local unfiltered water supply. This in turn might be lowering the intake of natural water, the necessary activity to promote health throughout the body. Water in its pure form and consumed on a daily basis, throughout the day, enables the body to maintain optimum health. It has been proven that water:

- Aids in purifying cells.
- Eliminates waste.
- Increases blood flow.
- Helps in the absorption of oxygen.
- Lowers fevers.
- Eliminates toxins in arthritic joints.
- Removes unoxidised sugar in people with diabetes.

- Helps constipation.

- Flushes the system at times of illness.

- Stimulates the liver and kidneys for filtration and the removal of toxic waste.

In order to understand fully the power of water I suggest you obtain no less then three books on water therapies. In them you will discover what healers have known for ages – that water is the cure for many illnesses; that it plays a part in all healing modalities for the body and our planet, Mother Earth.

Get into the practice of offering filtered water to your clients halfway through a LaStone session, and at the end of each session supply the client with a full bottle of filtered water. They can drink this while they are sharing their experience of the treatment with you, which should give them plenty of time to consume the whole bottle and to fully come back to reality before they have to walk into the rest of their day. I also hand clients a packet of Emer'gen-C by Alacer Corp., which can be found in many health food shops. This powder supplies the body with the necessary vitamins and minerals it needs after it experiences a loss in fluids through perspiration and massage modalities.

As it is for your client, so it should be for you. Water is the source of energy and filtration for our bodies. As a therapist it is important for you to be hydrating yourself with pure water throughout the day and during each LaStone session you are giving. Water not only filters toxins from your body, but also removes any energies you are not willing to hold on to. So drink water, pour cool water over your hands and rinse your face in water after you have finished each session with a client. Clear the treatment from your own energy field, so that you will be free to move forwards in your day.

One of the best books to read about the importance of water is *Your Body's Many Cries for Water* by Dr Batmanghelidj. There are many books on the subject of hydrotherapy; one of the best on the history of hydrotherapy is *Lectures in Naturopathic Hydrotherapy* by Wade Boyle and Andrei Saine – you will probably only find this book in secondhand bookshops because it is no longer in print. *Edgar Cayce's Massage Hydrotherapy & Healing Oils* by Joseph Duggan and Sandra Duggan has valuable information for the massage therapist. Another useful book is *The Complete Book of Water Therapy* by Dian Dincin Buchman. I refer to this book often for conditions that require precise usage of heated and chilled applications of water to the body. Finally *Water Detox* by Jane Scrivner is always a great book to have around (we would say that, wouldn't we!).

A Treatment for Everyone – LaStone Therapy

LaStone therapy is safe for almost every client. There are so many variables to the treatment that with your information, knowledge and intuition, you will be able to design a treatment that will suit any condition you are likely to come across. After asking relevant questions from your case history or in-take form, you can begin to make decisions on how your treatment will go.

Remember: you have several variables that you can take into account:

- You can use less time.

- You can use less temperature.

- You can use fewer stones.

Variable Temperatures and Duration of Temperatures

The results of a LaStone treatment depend on the temperature and the duration of the various temperatures and how they are applied to the client's body. Below are examples of the different temperatures of a heating or chilling unit. It is important to also understand that these are not the temperatures of the stone(s). A unit maintains the temperature of the stones while the stones are still within it. Within seconds of being removed from the unit, a stone begins to loose that specific temperature. When simply placed on the body, as in a chakra or spinal layout, a stone will continue to supply varying degrees of temperature to the body for about twenty to thirty minutes. When a stone is applied to the body over bare skin, the stone gives up its temperature very quickly to the body – this period of time is about thirty to sixty seconds, a big difference in duration of exposure to temperature.

POSSIBLE VARYING DEGREES FROM BODY CORE TEMPERATURES

Chilling Unit Temperature	Body Temperature	Heating Unit Temperature
25°F/-4°C	98°F/37°C	140°F/60°C
32°F/0°C	98°F/37°C	135°F/57°C
40°F/4°C	98°F/37°C	130°F/54°C
50°F/10°C	98°F/37°C	120°F/49°C
Room temperature	98°F/37°C	110°F/43°C

Note: ice with a little water is 32°F/0°C degrees.

Examples of How this Chart Might Work

If, for instance, your client has a contraindication that requires you to lessen the amount of time you offer temperature to the body, and to use a lower temperature within the range of a temperature being offered:

- **First week**
  Less time and lower temperature: you may choose to start with 110°F/43°C for thirty minutes.

- **Second week**
  Increase the time to forty-five minutes and maintain the temperature at 110°F/43°C.

- **Third week**
  Increase the time to sixty minutes and the temperature to 120°F/49°C.

The increase in time and temperature will be determined by the results of the treatments. If a client responds favourably you can slowly increase the time and then the temperatures being applied to them each week. If their response is not favourable you will need to adjust the time and temperature to support the treatment of choice. As a care provider it should be your goal to strengthen and tonify the body. You can do this by controlling the temperature and the amount of time you apply temperature to the body. The only way to know when you can increase the length of a treatment and the degrees within that session is by monitoring the results of your client within a seventy-two-hour time frame.

Whatever your client's condition, we are creating *balance* within the body with LaStone. We just need to think about how far our clients are currently away from their place of perfect balance and how quickly they can cope with getting back to this place. If they are very fit and a little out of balance we can probably challenge their body with no problems. If they are very ill, or badly out of balance, we need to be very much more gentle towards them and take it slowly. They will get there but it will take a few more treatments and a little longer.

One way to think about what type of treatment, temperature, duration and placement you will use is to consider what sort of exercise the client could manage in their current condition. Quite simply, I ask myself whether

I would I take them for a run, jog or walk, or just sit with them on a bench in the park.

Bearing in mind the list of contraindications and considerations, it is easy to see how one might think this treatment may not be possible in its entirety for many people. However, virtually everyone can benefit from some level of LaStone therapy.

Condition of Client	My Treatment
If the client can go to the gym for a full hour's workout as normal and then take a hot and ice cold shower.	I will do the whole treatment in its entirety with heated and chilled stones at maximum temperature – no problems here.
If they can take a beginner's aerobics class and have a good rest afterwards before getting into the shower to cool off – face still red after shower!	The whole treatment will be fine but will perhaps be conducted at 5 degrees less – 135°F or 55°C.
If they are able to go for a light jog around the block but at a gentle pace and taking a rest on the bench.	I will maybe provide a 45-minute treatment at first but using normal temperature.
If they have never done any exercise except housework and if the only time their pulse gets going is when they are stressed.	I will do a 45-minute treatment with temperature reduced further and ask them regularly if they are feeling good.
If they have not been well, are elderly or are not in good shape, and if a walk in the park can take their breath away.	I will perhaps just do 'castle building' (*see page 169*) – remembering that this com prises perfect delivery of temperature with the energy of the stones but is seemingly less 'active' for the client. Take about 45 minutes and check in with them – if they are still awake!
If they have never done any exercise and never had a massage, and if a walk to the corner shop makes them out of breath.	I will provide a treatment for 30 minutes with reduced temperature, gentle massage and gentle thermotherapy.

We know that at the end of the day we are creating balance, and that can only be beneficial, but we have the choice of the journey there being an uphill adventure or a different and less tricky route!

Indications and Contraindications

The following is a small list of reasons why one might choose to use both heated and chilled stones in treatments. I personally alternate between the two temperatures on everyone.

Indications for short-term cold only

Sprains, strains, acute bursitis, chronic tension, acute inflammation, tennis elbow, toothache, headache, fever, sunburn, cerebral congestion, bowel inflammation, constipation, bruises, insect bites, atrophied muscles, osteomyelitis, varicose veins, menstrual cramps and just because the treatment feels so incredible.

Contraindications

There are always considerations within a treatment using alternating temperatures. Anyone can receive some form of LaStone therapy; the art is in designing a treatment that best suits your client's needs for the day. Read all the charts that follow to begin to understand the parameters of how you can offer temperatures to your client's body.

Reddening of the skin – is it quite normal?

LaStone therapy utilises both heated and chilled stones within a treatment to create new circulation patterns that relieve congestion in many internal organs. The red marks that may be present after a LaStone treatment are caused by a rapid increase of blood flow to an area. The heat brings the blood into the tissue to relax and soften tight, congested structures. These areas should return to a normal skin tone within the time of the treatment or shortly thereafter.

If an area remains red, this is an indication that it is very congested and needs some extra work. It could be congestion in the muscle's structure or the underlying organ, or energetic or meridian blockages. There is no need for alarm. In fact, this is usable information for the therapist and client, for it indicates that these are the key areas on which to focus your attention. Applying extreme temperatures in and around these areas will assist in loosening the congested tissue. Educate your clients before they leave your treatment room in regard to these 'road maps' with an intention to focus on these areas in upcoming sessions.

The chilled marble stones will sometimes leave a slight red mark as well. This is due simply and solely to the fact that the client has lain on them for an extended period of time. This is similar to falling asleep with your hand against your face, and an 'imprint' is left due to the pressure alone. These marks disappear immediately after the stones are removed from the area. They are not created by the same internal response as the marks left by the heat.

Some common contraindications and considerations

1. Any places where there has been surgery and nerves have been cut: usually there's a loss of feeling in these areas, especially in the back region, and the client may not register correct temperatures in these places.

2. Any disease where there is nerve damage or neuropathy, diabetes, etc.

3. Any skin conditions, which may be aggravated by moisture or heat.

4. Pregnancy – heat is the variable to be concerned with. In the hands of a highly skilled therapist or hydrotherapist, treatment can be adapted to a safe application.

5. Anyone on prescription medications that may have side-effects due to the heat or temperature challenges. All individuals who are not sure of their medication should consult their doctor.

6. Heart disease – temperatures challenge the circulatory system.

7. Anyone who is considered 'overweight or obese' may be challenged owing to the stress on the heart.

8. Anyone you perceive as underweight may be challenged owing to the lack of muscle density.

9. Anyone in a very weak and/or debilitated state before the treatment begins – where the body cannot balance itself after being challenged by the temperatures.

10. Varicose veins – heat is not good; cold is very beneficial.

11. All autoimmune dysfunctions such as chronic fatigue syndrome, Epstein Barr syndrome, AIDS and cancer in their acute and worst conditions, where the immune system is already taxed.

12. Exercise caution when there is epilepsy, depression and mental disorders; any condition where the brain and nervous system are challenged – alternating temperatures may affect brain activity.

13. The thin skin of the elderly or someone taking cortisone medications should be dealt with carefully, using lighter pressure and less extreme temperatures than you would normally use.

14. Young children need very little to stimulate their systems; they require less time and less extreme temperatures. If a child is under the age of ten, I ask the parent/guardian to take the child's bath-water temperature. Then I raise the heating unit temperature five degrees above the child's normal bath water, and I adjust the marble stones to fit the heating unit's temperature as well.

15. In any condition where Swedish massage is contraindicated, the application of heated and chilled stones will enhance the body's response to the treatment. In this case I design an energy treatment involving alternating temperatures and avoid all Swedish massage applications to the body.

After reading the list of contraindications you might feel less confident about giving a LaStone treatment to anyone with one or more of these conditions. However, by following some of the basic principles of temperature application, many of these conditions can be addressed safely. First and foremost you must have as much information as possible regarding your client's health. By understanding and following the two primary rules of geothermotherapy, most conditions can be treated safely and effectively. Remember that the results of your treatment are going to depend on two main things: the temperature being applied and just as importantly the duration of that temperature. As the body strengthens, so the treatment becomes stronger. As a client becomes healthier they will be able to tolerate a treatment of more extreme temperatures and duration without negative reactions. Hence: 'less is more'.

Possible negative reactions to a treatment

Arterial: too lengthy an application of chilled stones or abrupt contrasts between heated and chilled temperatures – muscle spasm.
Stop the treatment, and carefully add warm/heated stones to the feet.

Venous: too lengthy an application of warm/heated stones – dilation of the veins, leading to venous congestion.
Stop the treatment, dry off the affected limbs and raise and exercise them.

Arteriosclerosis: contradictory reaction to what should occur when heat is applied – the body reacts as if cold has been applied, and takes on a blue-white appearance.
Stop the treatment and alert the client's doctor.

Geothermotherapy charts for reference purposes, from Mary Nelson:

The following charts are designed to give you ideas and suggestions as to how you can offer geothermotherapy practices via a LaStone session. They are not exact methods of applying temperature to the body for any particular condition or concern. They are the results of my experiments and research on hydrotherapy, aimed at bringing about a chemical response in the hopes of promoting and encouraging health and well-being. I offer these charts to you as guidelines only: it is my hope that you will monitor, record and grow with all your client's responses in order to develop your own path with temperature and with Mother Earth's vibration offered to the body via the stones.

In many cases you will choose to do shorter or longer versions of LaStone therapy. The reason why you choose to lessen the amount of time spent on offering alternating temperatures to the body will depend on the condition of the client and their concerns. This will be determined by examining the in-take form your client fills out for you and/or by discussing what their goals are for the day. It may be necessary for you to consult your client's doctor in order to create a treatment that will best serve their needs.

The chart below shows how far away from body-core temperature the chilled and/or heated stones can be. The amount of time spent on using chilled and heated stones on the body at any of these varying degrees will be determined by the strength of the client's body at the time of treatment. The weaker the body is the less time you can spend using geothermotherapy practices; the stronger it is the longer you can apply alternating temperatures to it. If in doubt it is best to carry out a treatment for less time and to use less extreme temperature for the first few sessions. A stronger treatment with an increase in time and then in temperatures can be developed over a period of time. This will enable the body to tonify and strengthen over a period of time, and will give longer lasting results with less of a possibility of side-effects.

It is also important to keep in mind that the exact temperature of a stone at any given time depends on whether you are massaging (convection), or placing the stones (conduction) on the chakras or during the spinal layout, or tucking stones in isolated areas. Do keep in mind how rapid a stone alters in core temperature by the act of convection and how it may hold its temperature for a longer period of time in the process of conduction. Having all this information, be mindful while using alternating temperatures. I hope that the following charts help to shed some light on why LaStone therapy is such a powerful treatment

EXAMPLES OF RESPONSES TO HEATED STONES OVER ISOLATED AREAS

Isolated Area	Body's Response
Bladder	Prolonged application over the pelvic region relaxes the muscles within the bladder/uterus, dilates blood vessels and relieves spasms.
Bowel	Prolonged application decreases peristalsis and relieves spasms.
Brain	Long application sedates mental activity.
Heart	Prolonged application over the heart helps to lower blood pressure.
Kidneys	Prolonged application relieves pain due to spasms.
Lungs	Prolonged application over the chest and lung area slows respiration.
Muscles	Prolonged application softens and relaxes the muscles, allowing for more intense massage work for a longer period of time.
Nervous system	Short application is stimulating.
Pelvis	Short application around the groin, pelvis or inner thighs dilates the blood vessels of the pelvic organs and relaxes this region for deeper work.
Stomach	Long-term application over the stomach or solar plexus area after a meal slows down digestion and decreases gastric secretions. Prior to a meal it will increase gastric secretions.
Thyroid	Prolonged application over the thyroid increases vascular and glandular activity.
Uterus	Short application causes dilation of blood vessels; relaxing the muscles.

EXAMPLES OF RESPONSES TO CHILLED STONES OVER ISOLATED AREAS

Isolated Area	Body's Response
Bladder/uterus	Short application causes contraction of muscles; can be applied to hands or feet to affect the organs.
Bowel	A cold application will increase peristaltic movement.
Brain	Short application stimulates mental activity. Prolonged application to the hands causes contraction of vessels to the brain.
Heart	Prolonged application over the heart causes contraction of the artery and its furthest branches. Caution: cold stones applied over the carotid artery decrease blood flow to the brain.
Kidneys	Short application intermittently to sternum will increase urination.
Lungs	Short application at first increases respiration, and after a few minutes may slow down respiration.
Muscles	Short application to isolated muscles increases the range of motion and muscle ability, is stimulating and reduces inflammation
Nasal mucous membranes	Prolonged application in hands can overcome a nosebleed.
Nervous system	Short application of cold stones is stimulating.
Pelvis	Prolonged application of cold stones to groin, pelvis or inner thighs contracts the blood vessels of the pelvic organs.
Stomach	Short-term application over the stomach or solar plexus area after a meal speeds up digestion and increases gastric secretions. Prior to a meal long-term application will slow down gastric secretions, allowing you to go longer between meals.
Thyroid	Prolonged application over thyroid decreases vascular and glandular activity.
Uterus	Short-term application causes constriction of blood vessels and the muscles. Prolonged application dilates blood vessels; this in turn increases menstrual flow and lessens pain and cramping.

Alternating Temperatures and Duration of Exposure to Specific Temperatures in Acute and Chronic Conditions

Acute conditions

The term acute is used to refer to a condition that has a rapid onset and severe symptoms, and does not last for more than a few days. Start with the application of chilled stones in the isolated area of the acute condition. Alternate between chilled and heated stones. The final application will be with chilled stones.

Application	Number of Stones	Duration	Stone Placement/tuck	Massaging with Stones on Acute Area
Chilled	2 sets	2 minutes	Yes	No
Heated	1 set	1 minute	Yes	No
Chilled	2 sets	2 minutes	Yes	No
Heated	1 set	1 minute	Yes	No
Chilled	2 sets	2 minutes	Yes	No

Chronic conditions

The term chronic denotes a condition that is long term or frequently recurring, usually with the presence of inflammation. Start with the application of heated stones in the isolated area of the chronic condition. Alternate between heated and chilled stones. The final application will be with chilled stones. Any condition can be chronic and/or acute at the same time; if a chronic condition is inflamed (involving pain) at the time of treatment, treat it as acute (*see above chart*).

Application	Number of Stones	Duration	Stone Placement/tuck	Massaging with Stones on Chronic Area
Heated	2 sets	3 minutes	Yes	Yes
Chilled	1 set	2 minutes	Yes	Yes
Heated	2 sets	3 minutes	Yes	Yes
Chilled	1 set	2 minutes	Yes	Yes
Heated	2 sets	3 minutes	Yes	Yes
Chilled	2 sets	4 minutes	Yes	Yes

We all know how our bodies welcome heat and warmth to find comfort and security. Many of my clients comment on how 'delicious' the chilled stones feel on the different parts of their body that are inflamed and in need of relief: 'Like ice cream on a hot summer's day.'

In summary:

- Short-term heat is stimulating to the body initially.

- Short-term chilling is stimulating to the body initially.

- Long-term heat is sedating to the body.

- Long-term chilling can be relaxing to the body.

- The length of time you offer temperature to the body is very important.

- The degree in which you offer temperature to the body is important.

- Each treatment requires you to adjust the length and degree of temperature being offered to the body.

CHAPTER 12

LaStone Sequences/Stroke Sheets

KEY POINTS

- The following stroke sheets are to be used as guidelines and suggestions as to what you can do with alternating temperatures, vibration and the Stone People within a body session. They will be variations and combinations of what you learned during the practical sessions on your Original Body course. They are not meant to be used by anyone who has not taken the course with a qualified LaStone instructor.

- It is my hope that you realise that every soul that enters your massage room deserves a stroke sheet designed especially for them on that particular day.

- Keep it simple at first.

- Less is more.

- Remember that your client doesn't know your sequence, so they won't know if you make a mistake – unless you tell them!

- Keep your intention true and honour the stones; they will take care of the rest.

- (Oh! And study hard and become a really fantastic LaStone therapist!)

Some Stroke Sheets for Inspiration

Extremely basic Original Body prompt sheet

- Travel up the left and out the right.

- Work with the breath; place and remove with the breath.

- Place the client on the spinal layout (Bag 1 and any/or cold stones).

- Place a pillow under their thighs.

- Remove Bag 2 and/or any cold stones.

- Place at the end of the table by the client's feet/legs.

- Do spiral opening (heart to TP point, clockwise).

- Do energy connection, placing stones as you go (ankle knee, knee hip, etc).

- Start treatment.

- Massage the legs from the knees down, including the feet.

- Place the toe stones.

- Cover the right side, uncover the left side.

- Oil and massage the entire left side of the body with stones.

- Cover the left-hand side.

- Oil and massage the entire right side with stones.

- Cover the right-hand side.

- Take Bag 3 to the head of the client.

- Remove any stones in the way with breath.

- Massage the face, chest and shoulders with stones.

- Tuck stones as you go.

When finished:

- Remove the tucked stones and spare stones. Leave the chakra stones.

- Remove the chakra stones from the body with breath and place at the foot of the table.

- Do closing spiral (TP point to heart anti-clockwise).

- Clear all the stones.

- Remove the pillow.

- Choose a belly stone.

- Take it to the head of the table; sit the client up.

- Remove spinal layout.

- Place the belly stone on the table and cover.

- Turn the client over.

- Place all the stones back in the heating and chilling units.

- Place a pillow under the client's ankles in the prone position.

- Choose the sacral stone.

- Place the stone with connection (ankle, knee, etc).

- Massage the entire back of the body with stones.

- Either uncover all the body with the towel tucked centrally, or uncover each leg and then the back.

- When complete, cover the client and remove all the stones with breath.

- Do spinal spiral (nine circles up and away from either side of the spine, moving to the far side).

- Finish by cleaning the feet/hands.

Some wonderful experiences for your clients, from Mary Nelson:

Original Body stroke sheet: 90-minute treatment

Supine position

1. Greet your client.

2. Reinforce to the client that it is their responsibility to inform you if the stones are ever too hot. Explain that you can easily adjust the temperature to their comfort level.

3. Do any supine stretches you are skilled in performing.

4. Sit your client up.

5. Cover their back with the sheet that they are lying on. This will offer them security as well as a cover for the spinal layout stones.

6. Place a pillowcase behind them.
   a. Adjust the opened end of the pillowcase in such a way that it is standing up at the gluteal crease; this allows for added protection from the hot stones that will shortly be resting near the gluteus.
   b. The other function of the pillowcase is to assist you in picking up the spinal layout stones when it is time to remove them from behind the client, just before you turn them over onto their stomach.

7. Remove Bag 1 (twelve small stones, four large flat stones and the pillow stone) from the heating unit.

8. Drain Bag 1 at the workstation.

9. Bring Bag 1 (seventeen stones) to the massage table.

10. Gently dump the contents of Bag 1 behind the client onto the pillowcase.

11. Find the twin for each of the stones.

12. Holding your open hand at the top of the massage table to estimate where the client's head will lie, place the pillow stone below your hand (your hand spread out is about the size of someone's head).

13. Place the thinnest of the largest stones at the base of the spinal layout, tucked partially under the person's gluteus.

14. Place the other two thin large stones above that.

15. Place the thickest of the twelve small stones above that; these stone will support the lumbar area.

16. Place the thinnest of the twelve small stones above that; these stones will lie along the client's ribcage.

17. Place the final four of the twelve small stones above that; these stones will lie between the client's spine and their scapulas. These stones should be touching the pillow stone, completing the spinal layout.
    a. If the seventeen spinal layout stones from Bag 1 are too long for the size of the client's back, you have two choices. You can take some of them and place them alongside the lower stones to add extra comfort and temperature to the body. There will then be two rows of heated stones on each side of the client's lower torso near the gluteus and lumbar areas. Or try rotating the stones so that they are positioned horizontally rather than vertically in relation to the body. There is an exception to this option. The top four stones must be vertical in relation to the body to lie between the spine and the scapulas (not touching bone).
    b. If the seventeen stones from Bag 1 are not enough to fill in the length of the spine for the client's body, try layng the stones vertically end to end; this will offer more length to the spinal layout.

Note that if you want to exchange some of the heated stones for chilled ones due to any inflammation or condition that calls for chilled and not heated stones, you should remove the heated stones that you want to exchange for chilled ones.

18. Cover the heated stones with a pillowcase immediately.

19. Go to the chilling unit and remove stones of the size and shape you need for the spinal layout.

20. Place these stones on top of the pillowcase covering the heated stones.

21. Taking the sheet that is covering the client's back, cover the chilled stones.

22. Assist your client in lying down on the spinal layout.
    a. Adjust the row of stones to fit any curves the spine may have.

b. If there are chilled stones in the spinal layout, ask the client to take a deep breath and say, 'This may be cool.'

c. Take time to adjust the pillow stone and any stones in the spinal layout that the client feels need adjusting.

d. You can ask the client to move around on the stones until it feels just right.

23. Place a bolster under their legs at the knees under the sheet.

24. Remove the two hands stones from the heating unit and place them under the sheet, and under the client's hands. (These stones can be chilled if there is inflammation in the hands or wrists.)

25. To determine the correct temperature for each chakra, you may refer to the client in-take form and/or scan the body. The chakra stones may be heated or chilled, depending on the client's needs for the day and on any condition you may need to consider.

(Here are two examples of how this works. If a client has problems digesting their food, then marble will speed up their digestion. If they are hungry, a warm stone over the solar plexus will sedate their stomach and allow them to ignore the need to eat.)

26. Remove Bag 2 stones (six large stones, grandfather and third eye stone) from the heating unit and drain off the excess water.

27. Place the Bag 2 stones on the workstation.

a. Once you have determined what temperature each chakra needs, scatter the eight chakra stones on the massage table near the part of the body they will be placed on.

b. Do not place stones on the body at this time.

Note that if the third eye stone is to be warm, I cover it with an additional hot stone to help keep it warm until I can place it on the client's brow. This stone is so small that it will loose its heat fast if it is not covered with a warm stone.

28. Hold the client's ankles and ask them how the temperature is along their spine.

a. Adjust it if need be to their comfort level.

b. Ask them to breathe deeply. You also find your breath in the present moment, and establish a rhythm so that your breath and that of the client work as one.

29. If you are guided to verbally take your client on a meditation or journey into Mother Earth, begin to share this with them now.

    Spend a moment or two on this guided meditation.

30. Begin to perform the opening spiral, honouring the rhythm of the client's breath (*see page 72*).

31. Then do the energy connection (*see page 76*).

    Honour the stone placement, energy connection and the client's breath as you bring a small piece of Mother Earth to the client's body.

32. Once all the stones are on the front chakras the massage begins.

33. Start at the feet.

34. Oil up the lower legs.

35. Remove two medium stones from the heating unit and dry them off. These are loose in the heating unit (not in a bag).

36. Being mindful of the client's breath, rest the backs of your hands on the client's lower legs.

37. Apply the stones to the client's lower legs with a firm and constant movement. Use effleurage as you firmly move the warm stones up and down both the medial and the lateral sections of the lower leg.

38. Flip the warm stones often. This allows the warmest side of the stone to address the client's epidermis, adding temperature to the client's body and the less heated side of the stone on your hand, and preventing any discomfort to your hands.

39. Remember to flip the stones even if their temperature is not too intense for you to hold them. This allows the warmer side of the stone to be applied directly to the client's body.

40. When the stones have lost some of their heat and are comfortable for you to hold, tuck them under the client's ankles.

41. Remove one pointy stone from Bag 3; dry it off.

42. Take a few moments to slowly work this stone on the bottoms of the feet. (If you have learned about reflexology this is a good time to put that knowledge to good use.)

43. Replace the stone in the heating unit in Bag 3.

44. Remove one more pointy stone from Bag 3; dry it off.

45. Repeat steps 42 and 43.

46. Remove the toe stones from the heating unit and shake off the excess water.

47. Place one stone at a time between the toes:
    a. Start with the thinnest stone for the baby toe and work your way to the largest toe stone for the big toe.
    b. Be mindful of the temperature of the stones you are using between the toes. Touch your temple with the stones to see how hot they are before placing them between the client's toes.

48. Undrape the client's left leg and arm, exposing the lateral side of the body.

49. Oil up the leg, arm and lateral side of the client's body.

50. Remove two medium stones from the heating unit; dry them off.

51. Being mindful of the client's breath, rest the backs of your hands on the client's lower left leg.

52. Moving the stones firmly and constantly, apply them to the client's lower leg.

53. Effleurage as you firmly move the warm stones up and down both the medial and lateral sections of the left leg. Remember to flip the stones often as you massage with them. Glide up to quadriceps, massaging the heated stones deep into the muscles as you go.

54. Glide up and over to the arm and spread what temperature is left on this left arm.

55. Tuck the two stones near the waist or under the hamstrings.

56. Remove two more medium stones from the heating unit; dry them off.

57. Being mindful of the proper application of heated stones to the body (see step 47), begin using these stones on the left leg and work your way up to the arm quickly but smoothly, allowing the body to feel the incorporation of the heat to the leg and arm as one.

58. Use the two stones to do additional massage on the left arm. Raise the client's arm over their head to massage down their side, spreading warmth from hip to elbow.

59. As the stones lose some of their heat, tuck them wherever they will fit nicely and add warmth to the body.

60. Drape the client with the towel that is covering their body. Also use the flat sheet they are lying on. Fold the sheet over the top of them. I will refer to this as cocooning the client. It offers them a sense of security as you are focusing your attention elsewhere.

61. Repeat steps 48–60 on the right side of the body.

62. Remove the toe stones and place them back in the heating unit.

63. Cool the feet down with a cloth soaked in cool water, witch hazel or alcohol, or a chilled stone or two.

64. You can replace the warm stones or place cool toe stones if you like at this time.

65. Place a chair at the head of the table if you like to sit while doing face and neck work.

66. Place your massage oil to the left of the chair on the floor.

67. Remove Bag 3 stones (four pointy and two face stones) from the heating unit.

68. Wrap these six stones in a hand towel and place on the floor to the left of the chair.

69. Remove four pointy stones and two face stones from the chilling unit, if you have them.

70. Wrap these six stones in a hand towel and place them on the floor to the left of the chair.

71. Note the reason why all the items are on the floor to the left of the chair: this is so that when you stand up to your right to perform the closing spiral you will not trip over anything you have left on the floor.

72. At this time it is crucial that you stop, pause, take a deep breath and find yourself in the present moment.

73. Ask the client to take a deep breath.

74. Remove the third eye stone with breath.

75. Remove the higher heart stone.

76. Take a few moments to massage the face and head without oil in your hands.

77. Remove the pillow stone.

78. Remove any stones from the upper trapezoids and rhomboids (two to four of the spinal layout stones) – these would be in your way when you begin the neck and face massage with the stones.

79. Place all the stones you removed in steps 74–78 on the floor to your left. To help keep the stones separate from one another and make cleaning up easier:
    a. Keep the Bag 1 stones, pillow and spinal layout stones in one pile on the floor to your left.
    b. Keep the Bag 2 stones, third eye and higher heart stones in a different pile on the floor to your left.

80. Apply oil to the client's shoulders, back of neck, rhomboids, upper traps and chest.

81. Offer the warm pointy stones to the deltoids first.
    a. Remember to offer the warm stones to the body with the back of your hand first and with firm moving pressure along the area you wish to share the warmth.
    b. Then bring the stones to the area of the neck you want to focus your attention on.
    c. Use all the heated stones first, because they will lose their heat fast.

82. To begin the application of chilled stones to the body, remember to hover a chilled stone above the area to which you want to apply the cold temperature.
    a. Ask for a full breath and with pressure, but no movement, apply the chilled stone to an isolated area and say, 'This is cool' or 'This is re-freshing.'
    b. The chilled stones should not be moved on the onset of application.

    c. The chilled stones need to rest on a localised area to allow the 'blood soldiers' (*see page 128*) to have enough time to respond to what is happening in the area of application.

    d. Use the chilled stones in the areas of inflammation, tension, and chronic and acute pain.

83. You may also offer temperature to the face with both heated and chilled stones, keeping in mind the nine rules of LaStone therapy (*see page 94*).

84. Complete the stone application to the neck and face.

85. With respect for all that you just did, stand up and begin the closing procedures for the supine side of the body.

86. Stand to your right and begin to remove the chakra stones (Bag 2 stones, or chilled stones) from the front of the body.

    a. The order in which you remove these stones is not as important as honouring the breath of the client.

    b. Match the rhythm of the breath with your removal of the stones so this becomes a dance to the soul. The mind will also better accept the separation of the stones from the body.

    c. Seal each area of the body that you remove a chakra stone from by holding your left hand gently on this area.

    d. Bear in mind that the act of 'sealing' is very important for your client. You have just removed part of Mother Earth from their body. The temperature and vibration the stones have been offering to them are now removed, and this can be shocking to them. This is why taking time to 'seal' each area and infusing love into the chakra before moving on to the removal of the next stone is so important.

87. Perform the closing spiral to seal this session into the client's heart centre with love and appreciation for the time you shared together.

88. Pick up all the items left on the floor to the left of your chair.

89. Remove any stones you have tucked under or near the legs or bolster.

90. Gently place your client's hands over their heat centre to hold the towel in place.

91. With breath assist your client in sitting up.

92. Quickly remove all the chilled or tucked stones from the top sheet.

93. Cover the client's back with the top sheet to offer a sense of security and warmth.

94. Offer the client water to drink while they are sitting up for a moment or two.

95. Remove all the stones from behind your client. These stones are the spinal layout stones (Bag 1), pointy stones (Bag 3) or possibly tucked stones.

96. Adjust the face cradle.

97. Remove the warm grandmother stone or a chilled stone for the abdomen from the unit and dry it off.

98. Remove the sheet that is covering the client's back and put it back in place on the massage table.

99. Set the heated grandmother stone or chilled stone halfway between the top of the massage table and the client's gluteal area.
    a. This will be just about the correct location for the stone to be lying when the client turns over.
    b. Cover the heated grandmother stone with a double folded pillowcase, or cover the chilled stone with a single folded pillowcase.

100. Turn the client over and adjust the towel. Place a pillow (king size is best) under their ankles under the sheet. Adjust the feet so they lie flat in order to support the placement of the stones on the bottoms of the feet.

101. Replace all the stones in the heating or chilling unit to bring them back to the appropriate temperatures.

Prone position

1. Take a few moments to do compression, rocking and stretching for your client. You will need to do this for about three to four minutes. It takes that long for the stones to reheat or to chill.

2. Cover the client's hands once and their feet twice with the sheet they are lying on.

3. To prepare the sock for the back of the neck:
   a. Use four small heated stones from Bag 1/spinal layout, or four small chilled stones.

b. Place these four stones in the sock so that they lie flat next to each other.

c. If you are using a sock tie a loose knot to hold the stones in place.

d. Set this near the client's right knee.

4. Remove the hand stones from the heating unit. Place them near the hands, not on them.

5. Remove the Bag 2 stones from the heating unit. Or use chilled stones of the same size and shape to replace the heated ones for the chakras along the spine.

6. Place the grandfather stone near the ankles or by the left ankle.

7. Place the two heaviest stones near the feet.

8. Place four large stones above the grandfather stone in a row along the left leg or between the legs (this will depend on how the client is holding their legs on the table at the time). Keep in mind that any of these stones can be either heated or chilled.

a. The combination is almost endless. It is all determined by the client's needs, contraindications, what temperatures were used in the spinal lay-out and most of all what your intuition is telling you.

b. There should be a total of nine stones and a sock resting on the massage table waiting to be placed on the body as you do the energy connection.

9. Holding the client's ankles, ask them how the temperature of the belly stone is. Adjust it if need be to the client's comfort level.

10. Begin the energy connection (*see page 82*) with honour to the breath of life, the Stone People and the process of this session you are partaking in with this soul at this time. As you place each stone on the feet and hands, on the sacral, spleen/naval, solar plexus, heart, higher heart areas, and on the throat chakra be mindful of the breath and rhythm of life within this being.

11. Bring the massage oil to the massage table.

12. Undrape the client's left leg, left arm and the left side of their body.

a. Bring the towel all the way to the stones that are resting on their spine.

b. The stones will hold the towel in place and allow you to expose the full side of the client's body for oil application and massage with the warm stones.

13. Tuck the towel in at the leg.

14. Apply some oil to the left leg, from ankle to hip and back again.

15. Gently remove the stone that is resting on the left foot and using this now warm (not hot) stone, spread the oil more completely all along this leg from ankle to hip and back again.

16. Using the same stone do a moment or two of point work on the bottom of the foot.

17. When the stone is warm, rest it on the bottom of the bare foot (not over the sheet, but on bare skin).

18. Apply some oil to the left side of the body and the left arm.

19. Gently remove the stone that is resting on the left hand and using this now warm stone, spread the oil more completely all along the side of the body and the left hand.

20. Using the same stone do a moment or two of point work on the palm of the hand.

21. When the stone is warm, rest it on the bare hand (the sheet is not needed here).

22. Remove one stone from the heating unit and offer more warmth to this side of the body. Pause to do isolated work as you find areas that need your attention.

23. If need be, retrieve another heated stone from the heating unit and bring more temperature to this side of the body.

24. Cover the left side of the body with the towel that is draping the client.

25. Cocoon the client with the sheet.

26. Step to the right side of the client's body and repeat steps 12 to 25.

27. With breath remove the four large stones that are resting on the client's spine, leaving the grandfather stone on the sacral area.
    a. If any of these are warm stones, place them on the massage table.
    b. If they are chilled, return them to the chilling unit.

28. Remove the sock from the back of the client's neck.

29. Undrape the client's back down to the grandfather stone.

30. Using the warm stones you set aside at step 27, spread oil along the client's back and sides. If all the stones resting on the spine were chilled, remove two warm stones from the heating unit to offer warmth to the back.

31. Stepping to your right, slide down the arm and exchange the fresh warm stone with the one that is in the client's hand.

32. Bring the stone you exchanged back onto the body, maintaining connection with both of your hands and gliding up to the shoulder area of the back.

33. Stepping to your left, slide down the arm and exchange the fresh warm stone with the one that is in the client's hand.

34. Bring the stone you exchanged back onto the body, maintaining connection with both of your hands and gliding up to the shoulder area of the back.

35. With these two hand stones (remember you just exchanged them for fresher stones), step to your left and, maintaining contact, glide out of the right side of the client's body to the ankle.

36. Exchange the stones in your hands for the ones that are resting on the client's feet.

37. The stones that were on the client's feet will now go back into the heating unit. Put them in Bag 2 or place them in the heating unit side by side so they are together the next time you want to use this pair of stones.

38. Undrape your client's left leg and right leg so that only the sacral and private areas of their body remain covered.
    a. Tuck the towel down between the legs so they feel secure about not being exposed.
    b. This form of draping is important if you are to perform 'up the left and out the right energy flow' (*see page 69*) in a LaStone therapy session.

39. Remove two medium stones from the heating unit and bring them to the massage table.

40. Place the backs of your hands on the client's left ankle. Ask them to breathe. Remember the nine rules of LaStone therapy (*see page 94*).

41. With firm pressure and moving the stones continuously, glide up the left leg to the hip using long effleurage strokes and offering warm stones to the body.

    a. This stroke with the heated stones is like ironing fine linen with beautiful lace to manipulate around.

    b. The pressure must be such that it will not to burn the linen. The details must be approached with caution so as not to disturb the fine details of the lace adorning the linen.

    c. If you can keep this in mind as you manipulate the heated stones on and around the muscles and bones, you will succeed in applying heated stones to your clients' bodies in the appropriate way.

42. Gliding up past the leg onto the back, step around the head of the client and immediately glide out of the body down the right leg.

43. Effleurage up and down the right leg at least twice to offer additional heat to this side of the body. When doing the energy stroke, it is very important that you massage up the left and out of the right side of the body in one continuous movement/stroke, offering heated/warm stones to the *full* body all at once.

44. Stepping around the feet, again glide/effleurage up the left leg up to the back.

    a. If there is any warmth left in the stones you can massage the back with them.

    b. If not it is time to exchange the stones in the client's hands.

45. Step to your right, glide down the client's left arm and exchange the stones.

    a. Maintaining contact with the body, step to your left and exchange the stones in the client's right hand.

    b. Maintaining contact, glide out of the client's right leg to the feet and exchange the stones on the feet.

    c. The stones that were resting on the feet will now go back in the heating unit to be recharged with energy.

46. Repeat steps 39 to 45 at least three times.

47. Cover and cocoon the client, exposing only the area that needs special attention.

48. Begin to offer temperature to this isolated area.

49. If it is a chronic condition you are trying to help, you will start with heated stones.
    a. Then work with chilled stones.
    b. Then heated stones.
    c. Then chilled stones.
    d. Then heated stones.
    e. The final application will be with chilled stones.

50. While working in this isolated area you can incorporate any body therapy modalities you are skilled at performing, offering temperature to enhance the performance of such techniques.

51. If the condition in this area is acute you will start with chilled stones.
    a. Then work with heated stones.
    b. Then chilled stones.
    c. Then heated stones.
    d. The final application will be with chilled stones.

52. When you have finished offering temperature to an isolated area it is a good idea to reheat the whole body and bring fresh warm stones to the hands and feet.

53. To do this you will need to undrape the client as in step 38 and repeat steps 39 to 45 until the body is warmed and the hands and feet have fresh warm stones resting on them.

54. It is now time for the bud technique.
    a. Make sure the body is warm; the hands and feet should have fresh warm stones before you begin this treatment.
    b. This is a meridian stroke; it is not effleurage or massaging.
    c. This is an exact stroke going up the left side and out of the right side.
    d. If this is done correctly it is stimulating and sedating all at the same time.
    e. If it is done without respect your client will not like it and the result will not be a positive one.
    f. If you perform the bud technique with respect and understand why you do this, then this is a powerful way to bring your client back into their body and the present moment.

55. Remove three medium stones from the heating unit.

56. Remove three medium stones from the chilling unit.

57. Place these six stones at the foot of the massage table.

58. Hold one chilled stone in your left hand.

59. Hold one heated stone in your right hand.

60. Place the backs of your hands at the client's left ankle.
    a. With firm pressure and continuous movement apply both stones at the ankle and glide up the left leg.
    b. Glide up the left side of the spine (avoiding all organ areas).
    c. Glide off the top of the left shoulder.
    d. Walk around the head; flip the stones in your hands if you need to for your own comfort.
    e. Place the stones back on the client's body (the chilled stone first), on top of their right shoulder, and glide down the right side of the spine (avoiding all organ areas).

    f. Glide down the right leg to the ankle, and off the body at the ankle, not the foot.

61. Take note you do not do this on the arms.
    a. The chilled stone goes first.
    b. The heated stone follows.
    c. When gliding up or down the spine area it is best to hold the chilled stone on its side to avoid contacting any of the organs in this area of the body.
    d. Please understand that gliding chilled stones over organs can cause emotions to arise in your client and this is not the time to encourage that to take place. The bud technique is a Yang experience and is designed to bring the client back to the present moment, not to open up old wounds.

62. Do the bud technique with three sets of chilled and heated stones, up the left and out of the right *only*. You may try placing a chilled stone on the fingertips when you are complete with the bud technique.

63. Note that if you take advance workshops with us, you will learn other ways in which to offer this type of running temperature to the body. I strongly suggest that you become skilled and confident in performing the bud technique before you explore the more intense application of running temperatures all over the body of your client.

64. Immediately cover your client with the towel and cocoon them with the sheet.

65. With honour and respect, remove the grandfather stone from the sacral area of the body, and any other stone remaining on the body.

66. It is time to begin the spinal spiral (*see page 87*).

67. Retrieve your Chinese fluorite stone (or a neutral pointy stone) and bring it to the massage table.

68. If you are right-handed, stand on the client's left side. If you are left-handed you may switch the hands you use to do the circles and stand on the client's right side while doing the circles. Sealing at the end must be done as I have instructed in step 74 (see below).

69. Put the Chinese fluorite stone in your right hand.

70. Hold the index finger and thumb on your left hand at T-1.

71. Place the Chinese fluorite stone just below your index finger in the ropey part of the spinal muscles.

72. Begin the spinal spiral. Note: this techniques is performed all the way down the spine past the sacral and coccyx areas (*see page 87*).

73. Once you have completed the spinal spiral, hold onto the spine with both hands and walk around the head of the client.
    a. It is very important to hold onto the spine
    b. Stand on the right side of the client's body. You must do this in order to seal the work you just did on the spine whether you are left- or right-handed.

74. To seal the spinal spiral, it is important for you to hold/hover the first two fingers of your left hand near the coccyx.

    a. Hold/hover the first two fingers of your right hand at T-1.
    b. Wait for a breath from the client or a shift in the energy field of the spinal fluid.
    c. Maintaining your hold on the coccyx with your left hand, move your right hand to C-1.
    d. Again wait for a breath from the client or a shift in the energy field of the spinal fluid.

e. Maintaining your hold on the coccyx with your left hand, move your right hand to the crown.

f. Again wait for a breath from the client or a shift in the energy field of the spinal fluid.

g. This will seal the work you did while performing the spinal spiral on the client.

h. It is most important to seal this technique before moving on to the closing ceremony you have customised for the client today.

75. The final few moments of a LaStone treatment should be spent in ceremony, ritual, honour and respect for Mother Earth, the Stone People, the client, you and all there is in this universe. Find your own path with this; experiment and enjoy bringing your inner knowledge of love and compassion to this closing part of LaStone.

76. Clean the client's feet and hands off with a cooling agent that will remove any oil. I use a cool marble stone as well to stimulate their hands and feet just before I encourage them to bring their awareness back into the room.

Original Body stroke sheet: 60-minute treatment

1. Repeat steps 1–47 of the supine position from the Original Body stroke sheet.

2. Remove the left-hand stone from under the client's hand and massage the left hand with this stone; point work feels really good in the palm of the hands.

3. Repeat step 2 on the right hand.

4. Glide up the client's left side and hold their head for a moment or two, watching their breath; find a moment of peace for yourself as well.

5. Repeat steps 87–101 of the supine position from the Original Body stroke sheet.

6. Repeat steps 1–76 of the prone position from the Original Body stroke sheet.

Energy treatment stroke sheet: 90-minute treatment

1. Repeat steps 1–32 of the supine position from the Original Body stroke sheet.

2. Then begin the energy treatment of choice for the day.

3. Upon completion of the energy treatment repeat steps 87–101 of the supine position from the Original Body stroke sheet.

4. Repeat steps 1–10 of the prone position from the Original Body stroke sheet.

5. Then begin the energy treatment of choice for the day.

6. Conclude with steps 65–76 of the prone position from the Original Body stroke sheet.

Energy treatment stroke sheet (supine position only): 60-minute treatment

1. Repeat steps 1–32 of the supine position from the Original Body stroke sheet.

2. Then begin the energy treatment of choice for the day.

3. Upon completion of the energy treatment repeat steps 87–101 of the supine position from the Original Body stroke sheet.

4. The final few moments of a LaStone energy treatment should be spent in ceremony, ritual, honour and respect for the Stone People, the client, you and all there is in this universe. Find your own path with this – experiment and enjoy bringing your inner knowledge of love and compassion to this closing part of a LaStone treatment.

Fibromyalgia

Pronounced fi-bro-mi-al-je-a, this term is used for groups of common non-articular rheumatic disorders characterised by pain, tenderness and stiffness in muscles, tendons and surrounding tissue.

Many of my clients have this painful condition, and it particularly affects their backs; one client has it all over. Using the chilled and heated stones, we have been able to find a system that gives clients relief for days. The first time a person experiencing fibromyalgia receives the following treatment I can assure you that they will hate it and tell you that they will never let you do that to them again. However, when you check with them that night, on the next day and on the third day, they will report relief. So the next week you will begin again. I suggest that someone with this severe case of discomfort comes for weekly sessions. All my fibromyalgia clients possess their own sets of marble stones. They use them every day to relieve pain and inflammation in areas of tension and pain. The following stroke sheet is an example of a fibromyalgia treatment; I suggest you try it and see what results your client gets, short-term and long-term on a weekly basis.

Supine position: 60-minute treatment

1. Repeat steps 1–6 from the Original Body stroke sheet, supine position.

2. Use all the chilled stones for the spinal layout. Note that I use two rows of chilled marble stones; this means that I use no less then twenty-four chilled stones for this layout.

3. Place the front chakra stones on the body as fast as you can – NO energy work, NO opening spiral. Get those stones on the body quickly before your client jumps off the table.

4. Repeat steps 28–47 for stone application to the lower legs and feet.

5. Massage the hands with the hand stones.

6. Repeat steps 87–101; use a heated grandmother (belly) stone to keep the client's abdominal area warm.

Prone position

1. Place a pillow under the client's ankles and lower legs.

2. Place the hand and feet stones on the client immediately.

3. At this point it is necessary for you to know how to do skin rolling, muscle popping, the piezoelectric effect and trigger-point work on the back.

4. Using heated stones do skin rolling, pop the muscles, work every trigger point you can find and do lots of piezoelectric effect.

5. Make sure you exchange the hand and feet stones with warm ones as you work, keeping the client's body very warm and grounded.

6. Cocoon the client with the towel, the sheet and maybe even a blanket.

7. Undrape the areas of concern (usually the whole back).

8. Begin with chilled application in isolated trigger point locations.

9. Then spread the cool stones all over the areas that are inflamed.

10. Repeat step 4 above.

11. Repeat steps 8–9 above.

12. Repeat step 4 above.

13. End with a final application of chilled stones to the areas of need.

14. Cover the client with a towel, sheet and blanket.

15. Repeat steps 67–77 from the Original Body stroke sheet.

This treatment requires your full attention to your client's needs and keeping all other areas of their body warm at all times. As mentioned previously, the fibromyalgia treatment will not be liked by your client the first or second time you perform it on them. However, they will feel relief by the time they go to bed and will allow you to do it again. To be able to perform this treatment effectively you as a giver must be able to do this with love and compassion for your client. It is necessary for you to talk to them about breath, to breathe with them and to cry if necessary with them. The success rate of this treatment for my clients and myself has been profound; within this type of therapy I learned more about the muscles, what the body, mind and soul can tolerate, and how we can all come through discomfort and find a life that is free from pain.

Castle building (oil free): 30–60-minute treatment

If the client has any of the contraindications for Swedish massage, castle building may be the choice of the day; the treatment is also excellent for clients who have never had a massage, or who may be a bit leery about taking off their clothing. Remember to do all the stretches you feel are necessary before you begin to build your castle of stones on the client's body.

One or more forms of energy work may be incorporated into the castle building session. You may also include some massage strokes, such as trigger-point work, piezoelectric effect, holding, vibration, rocking the stones and toning at various stages within the process of building your castle on the body.

An oil-free session using the LaStone therapy techniques for castle building is a powerful tool to offer your clients at times of stress and confusion in their daily lives. A full massage may often include too much information for one's emotions to handle for the day. Sometimes simplicity is what is called for to unblock channels of energies bottled up within our bodies and mind. The benefits received from just lying with the stones, and experiencing the various temperatures, the vibrations of the stones and the rhythm of one's own breath, is all that the body and soul need to go deeper into a state of relaxation that supports the mind in letting go of the day's worries and obligations.

It is important to set the mood in your treatment room; choose your music to match where you are going to take your client on their internal journey of self-discovery through the vibrations and temperatures of the stones. Before you begin the session, take a few moments to connect to your spirit guides, allowing all your stress and concerns to fade away with each new breath you take into your lungs.

One of the ways I enhance the experience of the castle building is by taking the client on a meditation journey. I do this by softly talking to them about their favourite place on the Earth. To find this out I question them before we begin the session. Then, when the time comes, I begin to slowly conjure up and describe to them what they might see in as much detail as I can: what the sounds are like, the smells, what animals may be present, what the sky looks like, what time of day it is and so on. All the time I am doing this I am placing stones on and under their body, matching what I am speaking about. Example: if I am describing a sunset, with changing colours and the bright sun's last bit of glaze warming their face, I might be placing a basalt stone under their neck offering support, comfort and warmth at the same time. With a gentle voice I continue – in the cool night air, the stars peek through one by one peeking as the light blue sky begins to fade away. I might then place a chilled stone over the client's heart centre, offering a sense of the crisp night entering their awareness and taking them deeper with each description and stone placement along their body.

I encourage you to offer this form of simplicity in your practice. Also experiment with the gift of castle building on yourself, allowing your own worries and burdens to melt away with each stone that lies within your energy field.

EXERCISE

Close this book and write out the sequence of your basic treatment.

Have the pages containing the sequence coated in plastic and use them during the first few treatments as a 'safety net', so that you do not forget or panic that you might forget the sequence.

Store the pages by your heater – you can then slide them out easily and check them once your client is comfortable.

CHAPTER 13

Ritual and Respect

The ceremony of a LaStone treatment is wonderful and truly respectful. Do not underestimate your clients' abilities to be intrigued by, and enjoy the experience of, ritual in their LaStone therapy.

KEY POINTS

- LaStone values the gifts from the earth and the sky.

- LaStone is in perfect balance – Yin and Yang.

- LaStone observes many Native American values and rituals.

- LaStone observes that the stones were here before us and will be here long after we have turned to dirt and dust.

- A LaStone therapist trusts the stones to deliver the temperature and leaves the ego behind.

- Everything we have on this Earth comes from the Earth.

- We use sage for the ancient tradition of smudging.

- We use a feather fan to represent the element air and Spirit for spreading the smoke.

- We use an abalone shell to represent the element water for storing and/or burning the sage and sweet grass in.

- We use a Tibetan bowl to represent the element metal; it is used to offer vibrations to the body.

- We use a rain stick to represent the wood element and offer vibrations to the body.

Becoming a LaStone therapist will open your eyes to much more than the new therapy. LaStone therapy has a tremendous respect for Mother Earth and Father Sky. We use these elements to provide healing touch and to prolong our lives as therapists. We celebrate the fact that we are using these tools to be able to work and do more, and to enjoy all that we receive in return.

Everything we have comes from the Earth – even synthetic fabrics are derived from oil that comes from the Earth. Money in the form of coins is made of metal, and it comes from the earth; notes are paper, and they come from the trees. Glass for our windows is made from sand, which comes from the rocks; salt which allows us to live comes from the earth.

Mother Earth and Father Sky give us all that we need to survive. We only need to go and harvest our hearts' desires and behold, our Mother and Father bring forth clothes to protect us, food to feed us, warmth and sun to feed our bodies and beauty to fill our eyes and spirit beyond anything we can create ourselves. The people on this planet need to take heed. If Mother Earth and Father Sky are to continue to give birth to even our simplest needs, we must begin to honour them; to give back what we have taken so freely. We have polluted his air, caused diseases to grow in her waters, ravished their four-legged clans and smothered so many different clan peoples. How then can we continue to take from the table they continue to spread before us? We cannot continue to do this without honouring them and all their clans. If we truly come from the clay of the earth, then we are a part of our Mother Earth and all are brothers and sisters.

To honour Mother Earth and Father Sky is to recognise their gifts; to see and feel the healing powers that are laid before us to use. One need only listen to hear the call of one of the clan families, as they reach out to the humans. Each member of a clan is willing to teach the human clan their powers, so that they can heal each other. Each clan family – the plants, animals, minerals and so on – wants to be of service to the humans.

How are we repaying the clans for this endless service that they have all performed for eons on our Mother Earth? Why are we gifted with such a high place in this chain of life when we don't even honour our own role in the cycle of life? If we did act as true kings we would see to it that each clan was well provided for. We would hear their voices as they call to us to use them. We would know that the power of our energies was uniting. We would be worthy of a higher place in this universe.

So I invite you to take a moment each day and go outside and breathe the strength of Mother Earth and Father Sky into your body. Become one with the energy of the universe, giving thanks for what the day is about to offer you. Spread bird seed for the winged animals, feed the trees that shade your dwelling place and care for your stone family that is now helping you in your daily work.

LaStone therapy acknowledges that we are not in charge; that as humans we are part of the picture, not the central players. Just as we think we are top dog, Mother Nature and Father Sky kick in to remind us that this is not the case. They send a little too much snow, and we shut down. They send a few too many leaves on the line, and our transport system grinds to a halt. We garden every weekend in fine weather, only to find that the weeds – the plants from the earth, the only ones we don't plant and take care of – come back again and again stronger and stronger. They are Mother Earth's flowers and we think we can tame them – not so.

In Native American tradition the Stone Clan People (that is, the stones) were the first beings to inhabit the Earth. Native Americans therefore believe that stones, rocks and boulders hold the memory of every event that has occurred not only on the planet but throughout the universe. We are not for one minute saying that the Native Americans practised LaStone, but we are saying that their values and respect for the stones is reflected in our therapy.

We use their ritual of cleansing with white sage at the beginning of a LaStone treatment, and we add feather fans from the animal kingdom to the ritual. Smudging is a sacred tradition that is found in many of the indigenous cultures of the world. The common belief is that the smoke from sacred herbs can be used for purification and spiritual preparation. It can clear, ground and centre, and can purify before, during or after a treatment. It works on both the client and the therapist.

You can use many other grasses or herbs to 'cleanse' at the end of a treatment – sweet grass, frankincense, copal resin, lavender; in fact anything that is indigenous to your area or country. It is good to do and you should use your intuition as to how you wish to 'smudge'.

You can use Tibetan bowls and rainsticks to achieve vibrational frequency. Placing them on or over the body or holding them as they ripple or chime can be an amazing experience for your client as they return to the room after their treatment – not so much a wake-up call but a gentle coaxing back to this world.

You can simply wash the client's feet and hands, which is an extremely honourable thing to do for them, and you can use surgical spirit, rose water, iced water, essential oils or just clean fresh water for this purpose.

Ceremonial Tools for a LaStone Treatment: a Summary

- A **feather fan** symbolises the element air and Spirit, and is used in spreading the smoke.

- An **abalone shell** symbolises the element water and is used to store and/or burn the sage and sweet grass in.

- A **Tibetan bowl** symbolises the element metal and is used to offer vibrations to the body.

- A **rain stick** symbolises the element wood and is used to offer vibrations to the body.

- A **Chinese fluorite/selenite wand** is used in spinal spirals.

- **Labradorite** is for recharging all the stones at the end of the day.

- A **candle** symbolises the element fire and is used to light the sage and sweet grass.

EXERCISE

Look into your local or national heritage, and see if there is anything you can include in your closing rituals that make the treatment 'relevant' to your area or country. Examples are a herb or grass that is specific to your country, or a particular oil or fragrance that is relevant to your area or treatment style.

Terminology

There are some techniques and terms used in LaStone therapy that may not be familiar to you. Here are the details.

Many of the strokes in a LaStone treatment are easily recognisable from a more traditional Swedish massage treatment. In fact the greatest compliment a LaStone therapist is likely to receive is when a client asks if they have a stone in their hand or whether it just that their hand feels very hot. The secret to a truly great treatment is to make the stones, hot or cold, feel just as natural as the therapist's hands. It should feel to the client as if the therapist has very firm and hot hands, or very firm and cool hands. This indiscernable difference can be achieved through lots of practice.

Strokes and techniques

Effleurage consists of long gliding strokes, which are usually used to apply the oil or lotion at the beginning of each treatment. It is an excellent technique to use in connecting the whole body with one long stroke.

At the beginning of a LaStone treatment using hot stones, the therapist should avoid bony areas when the stones are fresh out of the hot water. Using firm pressure, the stones should be applied to the muscles; the stones should be turned every two to three seconds, and moved briskly until they have begun to lose their heat. Once the stones are no longer hot, but still very warm, the therapist should return to areas that were not addressed at the start of the stroke and begin specific work. When the stroke is completed a nice touch is to place the stones in the client's hands while they are still warm; this feels as though you are being 'plugged in' to little pots of heat.

Petrissage is the kneading, lifting and squeezing of the muscles in a rhythmical pattern. This stroke is best done with plenty of practice as it often causes stones to fall to the floor, an unpleasant experience for both clients and stones. Petrissage is used effectively in the massage to find those deep trigger points or tense muscles. Once the manipulation has been completed the therapist can choose a different stone and a more specific stroke to address the problem area.

Bud technique: this is a Yang experience for the client. The extreme temperatures applied over bare skin demand that the body, mind and nervous system stand up and pay attention. The concept of this treatment is credited to Bud Fisher from Rochester, Minnesota, in the United States. Hold a chilled stone in your left hand and a heated stone in your right. The left hand (chilled) leads and the right hand (heated) follows. Starting at the left ankle glide up the left leg and continue up the back just lateral to the spine and off the left shoulder. Walk around the head and continue the application with the chilled stone leading. Apply the stones at the right shoulder, glide down the right side lateral to the spine, then in a straight line off the right leg. This is a revulsive procedure. Note that if the basalt stones you use are too hot for you to move them in a straight line without flipping them, you can flip them as you travel around the head and/or feet; this flipping action must happen off the client's body. It is just as important that the chilled stone does not lie flat over the organ area of the back. Place the chilled stone on its side while travelling up and down the spine, avoiding the organs in the back region.

Cat pawing is as close to petrissage as you can get using the stones. Cat pawing is done by holding the stones flat or on their sides or ends while you cat paw them back and forth. This feels like a cat pawing at something while purring. Firm pressure is needed with this stroke on large groups of muscles. Warm stones are used, but the stones should not be too hot, as the stroke is slow and deep, allowing the full temperature of the stone to penetrate into the tight muscles – delicious and very comforting.

Vibration is holding a stone firmly in one isolated location on the client and pressing evenly up and down, creating a vibration within the muscles. Therapists sometimes have trouble mastering this technique, and one hand or the other may work better. Two stones that are still quite hot are held together. The thumbs are linked and the dominant hand is used to control the vibration. This method ensures that the stroke gets to the root of the problem. The stroke is complete when the therapist glides over the area that has been treated by using this method.

Stripping is a slow, gliding, very intense stroke that follows the length of a muscle or group of muscles from origin to insertion. The stones must be warm, not hot, to do this stroke correctly. The use of one stone for stripping is best. Incorporating the piezoelectric effect (see below) in this stroke, before or after the stripping, aids in even deeper release of tense muscles.

Piezoelectric effect (pronounced pea-aye-zo-electric) is a rhythmic tapping together of two stones or crystals to create a resonance of sound waves, a flash resonance of light and a burst of electricity into or over the body, for deep penetration into the muscles, bones and nervous system. This is usually done with two quartz crystals. We are more familiar with the technique when it is called ultrasound. The crystals in quartz are in line with one another, and this creates poles that in turn can generate the electricity that occurs when the two stones are struck together. The basalt stones are made up of unsorted crystals with many poles going in many directions. Our experience with this technique has revealed that the nervous system responds to the tapping in a dramatic way not only over the body, but also directly on a point of tension.

To release a stubborn trigger point, use two warm stones. Place one stone firmly on its end on top of the trigger point; take the second stone and hold it on its end as well. Begin tapping firmly the stone that is resting on the trigger point. Maintain a constant deep pressure into the muscle while the tapping or piezoelectric effect is being applied. The stones need to be as warm as possible without feeling too hot while they are held in one position.

Trigger-point work applies direct pressure on an isolated area for thirty to ninety seconds (or less, if the trigger point releases quickly). This technique has many advantages, not only for the client, but also for the therapist's body mechanics. Using a warm stone, find the trigger point (you may need to ask the client for help here). Apply deep, firm pressure on the area of need; maintain constant pressure for up to ninety seconds if necessary. The heat of the stone and the pressure on the trigger point will assist the muscle in relaxing and giving up the knot it has been holding. The results are amazing. There is no strain on the therapist's thumbs and wrists, and therefore no tension in their own hands while they work on the client. Here again, LaStone therapy provides an effort-free version of what is traditionally a hard-working stroke for the therapist. The therapist can maintain a trigger point with little or no effort, allowing healing and release for the client at no cost to themselves.

The secret is to remember that the stones do the work and the temperature takes it deeper. The therapist almost becomes the assistant, simply judging where the work needs to be done and what shape of stone is best for the job.

Friction is applied by the quick movement of the thumbs or palms of the hands to create added heat, permitting the therapist to work at a deeper level along the length of the muscles. Holding hot stones in your hands will accomplish this in less time and the heat will last longer.

Cross-fibre friction is deep friction applied across a muscle fibre instead of along the length of a muscle. This aids in breaking up adhesions between the muscles and the skin. Following the above method for friction, go across, not along, the fibres of the muscles. This is an incredibly effective treatment of very 'stuck or sticky' muscles.

Tucking the stones is useful when extra heat is needed in many places. After a set of stones has been used for a certain job on the body, the stones can be tucked under an area of tension. This will continue to warm the area, so that when further work in that area is required it will be heated and relaxed. Deeper work can take place if need be. Sometimes tucking the stones relaxes a muscle to the extent that the tension just melts away, and the work is done.

Holding or energy work is a treatment that allows energy to emanate to the client; it can be felt by the client as an increase in heat moving around the area being held. One of the first things we remember as children is holding ourselves after we've been injured, to apply our own energy to stop the pain. As therapists we can choose to remember this natural technique we were all given at birth. In turn, we can pass on energy to clients to enable them to channel their own tension and stress to release what is no longer desired in the body. Placing stones on the chakras and other areas of the body allows a client to feel cradled in heat. Removing the stones after they have cooled gives the client a feeling of release, as though heavy burdens have been removed.

Geothermotherapy terms

Increasing your understanding of geothermotherapy is important to the success of your LaStone treatments.

Alternate To use a series of alternating heated and chilled stones on the body; you use the heated stones three times more than you use the chilled stones. This is literally using vascular gymnastics on the circulatory system.

Atonic reaction An atonic reaction involves a lessening of tone in the entire body or a specific area, a decrease of muscle capacity and a general feeling of drowsiness, perhaps with yawning. It takes place following a long application of heated stones to the body.

Chilled stones These initially constrict the blood vessels, which is stimulating to the nervous system.

Conductive heat transfer This is what takes place when the stones are resting on the body and not moving (during chakra placement, the spinal layout and the tucking of stones). It allows the thermal energy to penetrate the body in an isolated area, concentrating its energy locally to bring about a response within the system.

Convective heat transfer This is what takes place when the stones are moving on bare skin, creating a micro-environment between the client's body and the surfaces of the stones. The stones transfer the thermal energy more rapidly. The stones will rapidly adjust their temperatures from hot/Yang to warm/Yin, or from cold/Yang to cool/Yin during this convective heat transference, or as massage therapists would understand it, during effleurage.

Derivation The drawing of blood or lymph from one part of the body by increasing the amount of blood and lymph to another part of the body.

Depletion This refers to the result produced by a derivative.

Diamagnetic This refers to the frequency that the marble and the sardonyx stones share with the body. This frequency emanates in a direct line, somewhat like an arrow. This is very important information for placing the stones on the chakras and along the spinal layout. The direct line of energy/frequency can be used to enhance the effect with the stones.

Energy, or thermal energy This is how temperature is measured in thermal dynamics. Within this book the term energy will be in relationship to temperature and not a modality.

Fluxion An increase of blood flow resulting from the use of heated stones in an isolated area or systemically.

Geothermotherapy Geo=stones; thermo=alternating temperatures; therapy= body modality of choice. Geothermotherapy was the name coined by one of my students, Mike Elliff, in 1999 during one my workshops in St Louis, Missouri. It is with his blessings that we use the term within a LaStone treatment and workshop settings. Geothermotherapy is the application of either heated or chilled stones to the body for the purpose of changing the physiological responses that are going on within the body to promote healing.

Heated stones Stones that are used to expand the blood vessels, and to stimulate the autonomic nervous system.

Holding This is a treatment that allows energy to emanate to and from the client. This energy is usually noticed by an increase in heat moving around the area being held. When doing holding I hold the stones until I feel a movement take place. Then I release the energy by removing the stones. The stones should be replaced in the water as they are removed from the client so that they may reheat. Note that when doing an energy treatment with a client whose clothes are on, the stones do not touch their skin; in these cases it is not necessary to clean the stones with alcohol when you have finished using them.

Homeostasis The condition in which the body's internal environment remains relatively constant, within physiological limits.

Hydrotherapy Part of the science or medicine dealing with the treatment of water to enhance healing and improve the quality of health.

Paramagnetic The frequency that the basalt stones share with the body. This paramagnetic frequency emanates in all directions from the centre of the basalt stone, similarly to our own auric field.

Retrostasis The pushing of blood or lymph from an area with a chilled application of stones.

Revulsive Term applied to prolonged application of heated stones followed by a brief application of chilled stones – for example during the bud technique, or when doing the whole massage with heated stones and ending with one application of chilled stones.

Rocking the stones Doing this back and forth on muscles while asserting firm to deep pressure will result in something of a cross-fibre friction stroke. This aids in breaking down scar tissue as well as tight or knotted muscles.

Specific heat A measure of a stone's ability to store thermal energy. Most stones have a specific heat of 0.24 to 0.28 BTU per pound.

Stone moving, convection As in when you are massaging with the stones or doing deep-tissue work. The extreme temperature of a stone, whether heated or chilled, will only last for about thirty to sixty seconds. Within that time frame, the stone will have lost or gained a sufficient amount of thermoenergy to be less effective than it was in its initial application to the tissue. This requires you to retrieve fresh stones from the heating or chilling unit often in order to maintain the extreme temperature response you are trying to achieve with geothermotherapy.

Stone resting, conduction As in spinal layout, chakra layout. The stones are placed on or under a client, with material protecting the client from the extreme temperatures of the stones. The extreme temperature of the stones, whether heated or chilled, will only last for about three minutes. However the stones will continue to supply a sufficient amount of temperature to continue to offer a chemical response from the body and the organs associated with the stone placement.

Thermotherapy The treatment of disease by the application of hot and cold to the body or specific areas of the body that are in need of a change. (From the book *Naturopathic Hydrotherapy* by Wade Boyle and Andrei Saine.)

Tonic Its action is recognised by an invigorating feeling, reddened skin (hyperemia), greater muscle capacity, expansion of blood vessels after their initial constriction, an increase in skin activity and increased respiration (brought about by a short application of chilled stones to an isolated area or systemically).

Toning Use this treatment when you are drawn to help your client on a very profound level. To start, hold two stones of your choice, breathe and as you feel the resonance of sound coming from deep within your own diaphragm, allow those sounds to emanate from your mouth. When you feel the need to remove the stones, do so. Move to the next set of stones. Continue doing this until all the stones have been removed. Remember to place the stones in the water as you remove them.

Vibration This is holding firmly in one isolated location on the client and applying even pressure, up and down, to create a vibration in the muscles. When doing an oil-free massage you will not be able to travel as easily along a muscle group doing vibration. Nonetheless this is a most valuable form of release. Vibration aids in relaxing the muscles as well as in coaching the client to breathe while you work.

Water The body's life force. The drinking of heated or chilled water, or water at various temperatures in between, aids the body in healing. The application of water to the body in varying degrees of temperature offers multiple responses, promoting and demanding a change within the systems of the body. The body is approximately 78 per cent water, which is something to think about.

Yang is masculine, is warrior, is releasing. A stone of extreme temperature, either **hot** or **cold**, *moving, as in effleurage, over bare skin,* initially creates the response within the sympathetic system that demands the action of the body to maintain homeostasis. If a stone with an extreme temperature continues to be offered to the body, and enough time is allowed to elapse while massaging, the Yang experience will soften and reach a state of Yin.

Yin is feminine, is passive, is receiving. A stone placed over or under a towel (not touching skin) offers a response within the parasympathetic system. The heated or chilled stone's temperature slowly penetrates through the towel, allowing a lesser degree of temperature to actually enter the body. In turn the client feels cradled and nurtured by the temperature, and not at risk, in those first few seconds of a hot or cold stone moving along bare skin.

All of these strokes can be used on a client if you use oil as well. I encourage you and your clients to experiment with oil-free massage. For myself and for my clients who are willing to travel along new roads, it has opened up many new doorways into healing.

EXERCISE

When you have completed the course and done nine practice sessions, choose a word each week and learn it. If it is a technique, try it and perfect it. If it is a definition, understand it so you can explain further to your client the intricacies of the treatment.

Keep learning!

Resources

Website: http://www.lastonetherapy.com
www.lastonetherapy.co.uk
Email address: Info@lastonetherapy.com

Further Reading

On stones

Jamie Sams and Twylah Nitsch, *Other Council Fires Were Here Before Ours*, HarperSanFrancisco, 1991

Manny Twofeathers, *Stone People Medicine*, Wo-Pila Publishing, 1996

Byrd Baylor, *Everybody Needs a Rock*, Aladdin paperbacks, 1985

Laura Murray, *The Spirit of the Rock*, 1995

Marilyn and Thomas Twintreess, *Stones Alive!, A Reference Guide To Stones for the New Millennium*, TreeHouse Press, 1999

James Wanless, *Little Stone Your Friend for Life*, Element Books Limited, 1999

Jane Scrivner, *LaStone Therapy*, Piatkus Books, 2003

Hydrotherapy

Wade Boyle, N.D., and Andrei Saine, N.D., *Naturopathic Hydrotherapy*, Buckeye Naturopathic Press, 1988

Dian Dincin Buchman, *The Complete Book of Water Therapy*, Keats Publishing, Inc., 1994

Joseph Duggan and Sandra Duggan, *Edgar Cayce's Massage Hydrotherapy & Healing Oils*, Inner Vision Publishing Co., 1995

Dr Batmanghelidj, *Your Body's Many Cries for Water*, Global Health Solutions, 2002

Mary Muryn, *Water Magic*, Simon and Schuster

Jane Scrivner, *Water Detox*, Piatkus Books, 2002

Energy work

Brugh Joy, M.D., *Joy's Way*, St. Martins Press, 1979

Barbara Ann Brennan, *Hands of Light*, Bantam Books, 1987

Melody, *Love Is In The Earth, Laying-On-Of-Stones*, Earth Love Publishing House, 1992

Caroline Myss, Ph.D., *Energy Anatomy*, Sounds True

Dolores Krieger, Ph.D., R.N., *The Therapeutic Touch*, Prentice-Hall, Inc., 1979

Elizabeth Clare Prohet and Patricia R. Spadaro, *Your Seven Energy Centres*, Summit University Press, 2000

Paula Horan, *Empowerment through Reiki*, Lotus Light Shangri-La, 1992

Massage-related

Deborah Ardell Hill, *Spiritual Gifts Spiritual Reflexology*, DAH Enterprises, 1999

Andrew Biel, *Trail Guide to the Body*, Second Edition, Books of Dicovery, 1997

Clinical Massage Therapy: Understanding, Assessing and Treating Over 70 Conditions

Monia Roseberry, *Marketing Massage*, Delmar Learning

Miscellaneous Supplies

The following items can be purchase through AML Stone Source (USA) and Stone Forest (UK) (see previous page):

- Heating unit (18 qt. roaster) found in most department/homeware stores.

- Lingerie bags, found in department stores near the hangers and ironing boards.

- Insulated gloves, found in any hardware shop or department.

- Thermometer, found in any hardware shop, 6-inch dial thermometer.

- Wooden spoon with holes in it, found in any kitchenware shop or department.

- Minnow net, used to contain the toe stones, found in shops selling fishing equipment.

- Spa oxidiser, found at spa/pool supply stores.

- Anti-bacterial hand cream, found in health care shops.

- For other AML Stone Source items see listing above.

Equipment List

Full set heated stones
Full set chilled stones
Heater for stones
Chiller for stones
Single bed sheets/linens
4 pillowcases
Pillow/bolster
Large towel for covering client
Massage medium – oil, cream or powder
Rubber/protective gloves
Wooden spoon with holes
Scrubbing mitt or pad to clean equipment
Sterilising solution for stones

Alcohol/surgical spirit for cleaning stones
Hand towel for holding/carrying stones
Net bags/socks/for sorting stones
Massage couch/table
Crystals for treatment
Sage for opening smudging/cleansing
Matches/flame/candle
Equipment for closing rituals
Consultation sheet
Water for client
Chair or stool – optional
Essential oils – optional
Client!

Index